7·95

A Practical Guide to

Teaching

Maths

Within the National Curriculum

Andy Bailey Lynda Townsend
and Mike Wilkinson

Published by Scholastic Publications Ltd,
Marlborough House,
Holly Walk,
Leamington Spa, Warwickshire CV32 4LS

© 1990 Scholastic Publications Ltd.

Written by Andy Bailey, Lynda Townsend and Mike
Wilkinson
Edited by Jane Bishop
Sub-edited by Catherine Baker
Designed by Sue Limb
Illustrated by Roland Smith
Photographs by:
Richard Butchins page 144;
Isabelle Butchinsky pages 5, 69, 70, 79, 80, 105, 106
and 143;
Keith Hawkins page 46;
Eric Johnson page 39;
Dave Richardson pages 15 and 16,
Nicholas A Spurling page 121.

Every effort has been made to trace the sources of the
photographs used in this book, and the publishers
apologise for any inadvertent omissions.

Artwork by Liz Preece, Castle Graphics, Kenilworth
Printed in Great Britain by Ebenezer Baylis,
Worcester.

British Library Cataloguing in Publication Data
Bailey, Andy, 1948–
 Maths. – (Practical guides)
 I. Title II. Wilkinson, Mike III. Townsend, Lynda
 IIII. Series
 510

ISBN 0-590-76234-6

Contents

Introduction

Mathematics in the National Curriculum

The National Curriculum was conceived and designed to ensure a programme of mathematical activity which has progression, balance and breadth.

This is shown by the range of study provided by attainment targets covering:

- number,
- algebra,
- measures,
- shape and space,
- the handling of data,
- the use and application of mathematics.

The majority of schools probably already support most of the aims and provide most of the content specified, and it will be for individual schools to determine how adequate their schemes are. They will need to decide how to supplement or reorganise their approach according to National Curriculum guidelines.

The National Curriculum offers a balanced programme of study which may necessitate some adjustments to present schemes. At present, pre-eminence is often given to certain aspects of number, to the detriment of other important aspects. This was observed even before the 1978 HMI report *Primary Education in England and Wales*, and subsequently referred to in a number of reports on schools by HMI, the Cockcroft Report, and more recently in *Curriculum Matters 3: Mathematics from 5 to 16*, which states:

'If mathematics is only about "computational skills out of context" it cannot be justified as a subject in the curriculum.' (2.10)

Where both teachers and schools have followed the content and progression laid down by a published scheme, they may now have to look afresh at their planning of mathematical activity. Certainly, the National Curriculum's programme of study and statements of attainment will be the governing criteria in the planning of activities and it is probable that teachers will now have to be more selective about their choice of material.

When schemes which respond directly to the National Curriculum are published it may be unwise to rely exclusively on such material, which may cover the content of the National Curriculum without fully embracing its spirit.

In fact, schools may find that some parts of the programmes of study are not adequately covered by their present schemes. Examples of inadequate coverage may be:
- Level 3, Attainment Target 2, 'appreciate the meaning of negative whole numbers in familiar contexts';
- Level 4, Attainment Target 4, 'know how to interpret results on a calculator which have rounding errors';
- Level 5, Attainment Target 11, 'use networks to solve problems.'

The use and application of mathematics may also be inadequately covered by present schemes.

Cross-curricular study

The documents so far available show that although the curriculum has been separated into 'foundation subjects', there has been an attempt to encourage cross-curricular study.

This is indicated by the similarity or interdependence of statements for different subjects at the same level. For example, Science Attainment Target 1 at Level 2 includes the following statement; 'Pupils should use non-standard and standard measures, for example hand spans and rulers', whilst Mathematics Attainment Target 8 at the same level states that 'Pupils should use non-standard measures in length, area, volume, capacity, 'weight' and time to compare objects and recognise the need to use standard measures.'

The necessity for cross-curricular study is stressed in the 'Non-Statutory Advice' given in *Mathematics in the National Curriculum*. 'Mathematics is a powerful tool with great relevance to the real world. For this to be appreciated by pupils they must have direct experience of using mathematics in a wide range of contexts throughout the curriculum'.

Inconsistencies

However, one does come across inconsistencies in the provision for cross-curricular study given in the National Curriculum documents.

The working parties and NCC were under severe pressure from the Secretary of State to 'deliver the goods'. Their efforts in producing such a quantity of work in the meagre time allotted must be applauded, but the insufficient time allowed for consideration, feedback and reflection has inevitably led to some mismatch between the mathematics and science documents.

Discrepancies occur where, for example, understanding of the 'meaning of negative numbers in context' is expected at Level 3 in the mathematics document, yet in the science document pupils are not expected to 'be able to measure using a thermometer' until Level 4. What better context exists for introducing negative numbers than the use of a thermometer? Indeed, it is the very example used to support the mathematics statement concerning negative numbers at Level 3. Further difficulties occur in using weather and temperature as a context for the appreciation of negative numbers. In science, children are not expected to be able to measure weather elements, including temperature, until Level 4.

Not only do inconsistencies exist between statements of attainment in mathematics and science, but there are also oddities within the mathematics document itself. For instance, the example given to support the use of unitary ratios (Attainment Target 2, Level 5) requires children to use a ratio of 1:50 for drawing a plan of the classroom. The example used at the same level in Attainment Target 8, to support the understanding of 'the notion of scale in maps and drawings', merely asks the children to draw a plan of the classroom on a scale of 1cm to 1m, instead of a scale of 1:100.

Framework

Just as science is an excellent vehicle for the development of various mathematical ideas and skills, many other areas of the curriculum offer similar potential. Art can be used to develop an awareness of shape and space; geography can develop notions of position, scale, measurement and the collection and interpretation of data; and technology provides contexts for the application of mathematics, for example in the use of measures.

The National Curriculum seems to offer a framework within which primary schools can continue or develop their cross-curricular programmes. Careful planning and assessment is needed to ensure that appropriate specified programmes of study are delivered within topics, themes and projects. Schools will no doubt develop means of ensuring that work of this nature meets the relevant criteria.

Parts of some programmes of study, however, will not fit neatly within a planned project or topic; they may have no obvious cross-curricular links. For example, many of the statements within the attainment targets concerned with algebra have a purely mathematical context.

Teachers should not be reluctant to plan activities which are entirely mathematical in nature. This is after all preferable to contriving links with other curriculum areas. The challenge presented to schools by the National Curriculum therefore is to identify existing good practice, suitable materials and methods of delivery, and to make necessary adjustments to their curriculum in order to ensure that children are engaged in a broad range of activities compatible with their abilities and interests. This is not a new challenge; the difference is that now more direction is being provided.

Programmes of study

The programmes of study leading to the attainment targets prescribed by the National Curriculum clearly set out where we should be taking children. The destination is clear, but there is ample room for manoeuvre along the way. Chapters two to six of this book show a possible route to the National Curriculum, using the levels of attainment to break the journey into easy stages.

As teachers we will continue to play a vital role in engaging the child's interest. Otherwise, however valid the programmes of study, they will not ensure progress and understanding. We must provide the spark of inspiration in order to translate the programmes of study into statements of attainment.

This spark can be provided in a number of ways. However, the elements illustrated below are of particular importance for achieving an effective delivery of programmes of study.

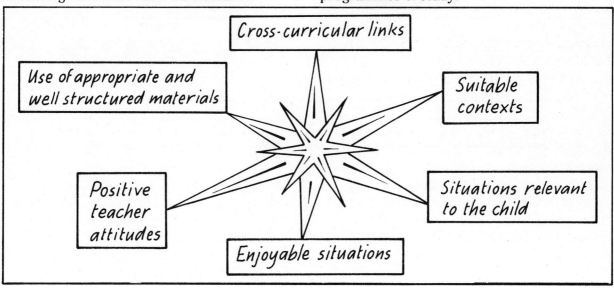

Above all, a positive attitude to mathematics is crucial to the acquisition of ideas, facts and skills. Merely adhering to the step-by-step delivery of schemes of work will not ensure that learning takes place; the children will be taken along a stipulated route, but they may not be absorbing the experiences provided by the journey. You must select interesting routes, including where possible some exhilarating landmarks! For this reason cross-curricular programmes of study have an essential role in providing suitable contexts for the development of understanding.

Cross-curricular links

As part of a topic on 'Houses', a group of five-year-olds was taken on an outing to a nearby building site. In planning the visit the teacher decided that among the many anticipated outcomes of the trip would be an opportunity to engage in activity at Level 1 of attainment targets 8, 10 and 11.

Adults accompanying the children were briefed on the opportunities for developing ideas and language about measures, position and two- and three-dimensional shapes. During the visit the appropriate language was used by both children and adults when describing and explaining the things they saw.

Under supervision the children were allowed to handle materials such as bricks and thermolyte, comparing their mass and size.

Back at school the children were encouraged to use appropriate language when handling the materials which had been brought back. The items were sorted and displayed according to a variety of criteria, and the children's findings were recorded. The children were also keen to construct their own buildings; while doing this they were encouraged to use appropriate shapes for specific purposes, drawing on what they had learnt.

Relevant situations

Many teachers have expressed concern over the statement at Level 3 which requires children to appreciate the meaning of negative numbers. This is expected to be achieved in familiar contexts. From an early age children using calculators are presented with negative numbers, and so a strategy is required to provide children with some understanding of this information.

Negative numbers were introduced to some eight- to nine-year olds who were particularly interested in football. They studied the total number of goals for and against various teams in the league tables printed in newspapers. Using calculators they recorded their results in the form of a table, as illustrated below.

This particular activity engaged the interest of the children involved, making the exercise meaningful and helping them to gain an appreciation of a concept which may otherwise have proved too abstract. The teacher involved understood that football was not of interest to all the children in the group, and other contexts were sought when required.

	Pl	W	D	L	F	A	Pts
Aston Villa	7	2	4	3	7	9	6	-2
Nottingham Forest	7	1	3	4	7	9	6	-2
Tottenham Hotspur	6	1	2	3	7	12	5	-5
Sheffield Wednesday	7	1	1	5	2	16	4	-13

Stage 1 Possible interest in the idea was assessed to see whether it was feasible, and if so what level of demand would have to be met.	**Level 4** ATs 9ABC, 12A
Stage 2 Sources of materials had to be found, and decisions taken as to which constituted the best value and what quantities would be necessary.	ATs 1AB, 2C, 3ABC, 4A, 8AB
Stage 3 Ordering materials.	ATs 1B, 2C
Stage 4 On receipt of materials, making patterns; then cutting out so as to involve the least waste.	ATs 1A, 8AB, 9A, 11B
Stage 5 Deciding on prices to charge for the fancy goods.	ATs 1ABC, 2C, 3ABC, 4ABC
Stage 6 Selling items and taking orders.	ATs 3C, 12A
Stage 7 Ordering additional materials and making up orders.	ATs 1AB, 2C, 8AB, 9A, 11B
Stage 8 Deciding what could be done with the small amounts left over.	ATs 1AB, 4A
Stage 9 Balancing accounts.	ATs 1AB, 3BC

Suitable contexts

At one school a group of ten- to eleven-year olds asked if they could make a positive contribution to fund-raising activities by running a stall at a school fête. They had previously been involved in their school's link with a local leather goods factory. They decided to make small fancy leather goods which could be sold on the stall.

This self-generated activity provided a very relevant context for various sorts of mathematical activity at each stage of the project. The following step-by-step account of the project indicates how relevant the various activities were to parts of the programme of study at Level 4.

Enjoyable situations

At every opportunity, mathematics should be presented as the enjoyable, rewarding activity it is. More able children will find a range of activities which afford such opportunities. For those children for whom mathematics presents a greater challenge you may need to create, use and exploit enjoyable situations in order to deliver teaching points. You will need to create an eager, enthusiastic attitude which overcomes any self-doubts or inhibitions. Games are an invaluable resource for creating positive attitudes. Keep them simple to understand, so that additional difficulties are not encountered by the child.

Following a lively discussion about a visit some of the first year junior children had made to a funfair, one teacher decided to back this up with a game from the school's resource bank. Using the funfair theme, the game gave children practice with addition and subtraction of numbers up to ten, and introduced them to the use of a symbol to represent an unknown number.

The board game 'Roller-coaster' was played in pairs, using a calculator. The children's tokens, representing cars, were moved along the tracks each time they correctly performed a mental calculation.

The number on which a token landed was entered into the calculator, and then the child had to enter a sum whose answer would be the same as the next number along the track. If this was successfully accomplished, the token could be moved along one stage. If not, then the token had to remain in the same place until the next attempt.

The children were encouraged to try to improve upon incorrect answers by, for example, looking at whether the answer produced was more or less than the target number. Errors were thus used in a positive way, rather than reinforcing any sense of failure on the child's part.

Positive attitudes

An important part of the teacher's role in the delivery of the National Curriculum will be to communicate ideas to children in an enjoyable way – enthusiasm can be infectious! The Cockcroft Report

recommended that teachers should use a number of elements in order to ensure 'successful mathematics teaching to pupils of all ages'; these are listed in paragraph 243 as:
- 'exposition by the teacher;
- discussion between teacher and pupils and between pupils themselves;
- appropriate practical work;
- consolidation and practice of fundamental skills and routines;
- problem solving, including the application of mathematics to everyday situations;
- investigational work.'

Following the introduction of the National Curriculum these precepts should still be seen as essential for the delivery of programmes of study.

Flexibility of planning and organisation will be required; some activities require children to work co-operatively in groups, sharing the tasks, collaborating and supporting one another. The group is defined not by proximity, but by the positive way members interact when engaged in a particular activity.

A useful model for evaluating the interaction within a group was suggested by Meyer and Sallee in *Make it Simpler: a Practical Guide to Problem Solving in Mathematics* (Addison Wesley, 1983). They hold that four roles must be filled to ensure optimum interaction:
- the questioner;
- the summariser;
- the prober;
- the doer.

In well-established groups each of the children will take on all of these roles whilst engaged on the task. This form of organisation is particularly suited to investigations and problem-solving in everyday situations, which are the forms of activity involved in Attainment Targets 1 and 9.

At other times children will be working on their own, or individually within a group of children at the same level. There is also no reason why a class as a whole, regardless of the range of abilities, cannot be set a single task. There will be opportunities for the children to respond at levels appropriate to their own ability.

Teaching materials

In planning and organising mathematical tasks for their children, teachers will still have a good deal of autonomy in the selection of suitable teaching materials.

In responding directly to the particular needs of their children, teachers often produce materials of their own design. In doing this they should be aware of the quality of the finished product – does it work as intended, does it engage the children's interest, and is it likely to be of value to other teachers? Create an accessible central store so that the school can benefit from sharing these valuable teacher-produced materials.

Money permitting, a plethora of structural apparatus is available to teachers, as a glance through any supplier's catalogue will reveal. Exercise some care, though, in selecting the appropriate pieces of apparatus to suit a particular purpose and the interest, maturity and dexterity of your children.

Published schemes have long provided the core of the mathematics teaching in many schools. Not only have they been the means by which the delivery of a mathematics curriculum has been achieved, but in many cases they have dictated the content, aims and objectives. This must now change, as the content is now dictated by the programmes of study. Used selectively existing schemes will doubtless continue to help put across many of the new components of the programme. The key factor here is to be selective and to relate the schemes to the programmes of study and attainment targets. It will be less advisable to rely exclusively on one scheme; it may in fact be far more effective to exploit the strengths of a number of schemes.

Consider the contribution which can be provided by individual books, as often these are written by experts within particular areas of mathematics. Also, a number of local authorities have produced guides and activity packs which are the result of the experiences of practising teachers. These often provide an excellent source of tried and tested, original material.

Planning mathematical activities

The aim of the subsequent chapters of this book is to provide a wide variety of material which can form part of a school's planned response to the demands of the National Curriculum. In the selection of activities the aim was to maintain a balance between the following criteria for planning schemes of work. Activities should:
- Combine different areas of mathematics.
- Maintain a balance between tasks developing knowledge, skills and understanding and those developing the ability to solve problems.
- Present children with opportunities to apply mathematics to other situations, in addition to working in purely mathematical contexts.
- Provide opportunities for both independent and co-operative work.
- Include both open-ended and closed tasks which demand different forms of thinking.
- Give opportunities for children to engage in a number of learning modes.
- Develop children's use of mental arithmetic.
- Develop children's confidence in their use of a wide range of mathematical tools.
- Provide opportunities for communicating.
- Develop personal qualities and a positive attitude to mathematics.

Some of the activities in this book are quite short, whilst others allow scope for development over a longer period of time.

Many of the activities can be used in assessment, as a number of them will be presented in ways which differ from the approaches adopted in main-line schemes currently in use in schools. They should therefore prove a more reliable test of children's progress than if familiar material is used.

The next section gives some guidance as to how this can be done, by explaining the format used for the presentation of material within each of the five levels of the National Curriculum with which this book deals.

How to use this book

Suggestions for mathematical activities at each of the first five levels of attainment are given in the next five chapters. Each chapter consists of activities relevant to one of the levels. An activity has been suggested for each of the statements at all five levels, but these activities are not intended to offer a complete course of study. Material has been selected in order to offer a wide range of contexts for the activities.

Topics

A number of mathematical activities can be incorporated into topics. In many cases, activities compatible with various topics as well as with the statements of attainment have been selected.

In order to show how a number of different levels can be delivered within one particular theme we have taken the common topics of 'Traffic' and 'Food', and have presented one or two activities appropriate to these themes at each level throughout the book. This may be of value if you wish to explore the same themes at all levels throughout the school.

Other curriculum areas

As it is not always possible or appropriate to link mathematics with topics uniting different curricular areas, other interesting and appropriate contexts have to be sought for some areas of mathematics.

Mathematics is a way of making sense of the world, so it is clearly integral to a number of activities in other curriculum areas. An attempt has therefore been made, when and where appropriate, to use other curriculum areas as a means of interpreting parts of the programmes of study.

Organisation of chapters

The next five chapters each deal with a specific level of attainment, and all follow a broadly similar pattern; an introduction, followed by two sections of activities (open-ended and structured), and then a glossary and three reference charts dealing with the relevant level of attainment.

Activities

The bulk of each chapter contains a description of the various activities suggested for that level.

Many of the activities suggested will be compatible with specific topics, and where relevant, suggestions for topic links have been made in the text.

The chapters are divided into two sections. The first part contains open-ended suggestions for use in various ways. The second section contains activities and games which are more precisely structured, and gives clear instructions for each activity.

Do not feel constrained by the fact that each of the activities has been allotted to a specific level; many of the activities may be adapted for use at several different levels.

Language

Essential language for the children is listed at the end of each activity, and at the end of each chapter is a glossary which explains some of the mathematical terms which are contained within the statements of attainment for that level.

Teaching stages

The first of the three concluding charts for each chapter deals with the particular Level of Attainment involved. This chart breaks down the programme of study into teaching stages, showing that the programmes of study do not in themselves constitute a comprehensive scheme for mathematics teaching. The programmes of study do not offer sufficient guidance for the achievement of statements. It is often necessary to identify appropriate stages within these programmes in order to ensure progression, and this is what the first diagram aims to do.

Contexts

The last table aims to show the different contexts involved in each activity at a certain level. If a variety of contexts is provided, a balanced programme of mathematical activity can be delivered to the children. Activities will usually have relevance to more than one of these contexts:
- Everyday situations which are familiar and interesting to the children.
- Everyday problems whose solution is likely to be of interest to the children.
- Games and situations which appeal to a child's sense of fun.
- Mathematical problems which demand a defined solution and make use of convergent ways of thinking.
- Mathematical investigations which have many possible solutions and make use of divergent ways of thinking.
- The use of a calculator.

- The use of a computer.
- The application of mathematics to one of the other core curriculum areas.
- The application of mathematics to one of the foundation subjects.
- The application of mathematics to 'local curriculum' priorities such as equal opportunities, multicultural education, safety, health or environmental education.
- The application of mathematics to religious education.
- Relevance to a topic.
- Relevance to school-wide themes such as 'Food' or 'Traffic'.

The 'Contexts' table shows how each activity is linked to these headings.

Attainment targets

The second table shows the statements of attainment which the different activities aim to address. Although in a few instances the activities set out to fulfil a specific or very limited number of statements, they can often be used in the attempt to deliver a number of statements simultaneously across a variety of attainment targets.

With the help of this table and the diagram which breaks down the programmes of study, teachers may find a number of the activities of use as part of their assessment procedures.

Chapter one
Level 1

Introduction

Every day in and around the classroom there are opportunities to engage in mathematical programmes of study. Young children enjoy playing within familiar contexts; they can gain much pleasure from games in the home corner or class shop. Their games can also generate a good deal of mathematical activity in a spontaneous and enjoyable way.

Learning at this stage does not fit neatly into categories – almost anything can become a useful learning experience. A child at Level 1 can learn about mathematical ideas from the simplest game, and the everyday activities outlined in this chapter will give rise to a number of mini-problems for the children to solve.

Level 1 sets the foundation for the rest of a child's mathematical education. New ideas and concepts can be introduced gently through games and situations which the children already find familiar, enjoyable and unthreatening.

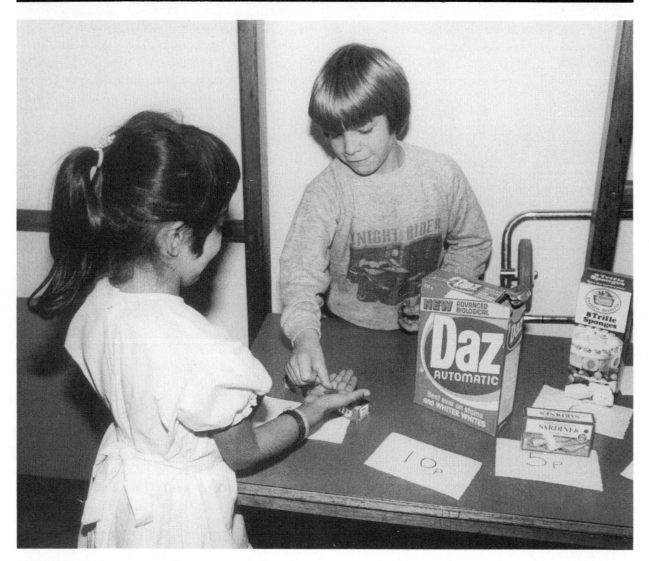

Classroom situations

Here are some suggestions for everyday situations which can stimulate mathematical activity at this level. They are by no means meant to be exhaustive; they simply illustrate how the sort of activities which regularly take place in infant classrooms can support programmes of study at an appropriate level.

Lining up to leave the room
The children will often have to leave the classroom as a group. It may not always be necessary on such occasions to line them up, but if it is, you can exploit the situation by introducing words for ordering and comparing; 'third', 'taller', 'behind', 'next to', and so on. Let the children try to compose a line of increasing or decreasing height. Ask them to copy, continue or devise repeating patterns when lining up. Try making a row of one boy, one girl, one boy, or sitting, standing, sitting . . .

Cooking
This is an activity familiar to all children and which many enjoy. Try to provide children with real cooking practice which will provide experience of measures and shape. Children will also generate their own cooking situations which in turn provide mathematical experiences. They might play at cooking in the home corner, or use Plasticine or modelling clay to make 'food'. If children are involved in the making of the modelling clay they use, they will be laying the foundations for concepts

of measurement at Level Two.

Home corner

This is a popular area in most infant classrooms and one in which imaginative or simulated play can involve mathematical thought and activity. Dressing up and laying a table are just two such activities and these can be used as contexts for teacher-child discussions concerning matching and counting, conservation of number, addition and subtraction, estimation, devising repeating patterns, comparing and ordering objects, sorting two- and three-dimensional shapes and describing position.

Shopping

The class shop provides children with another area where they can engage in activities which mimic the behaviour of adults, including scope for mathematical activity. In setting up their shop displays children could be devising or copying repeating patterns, comparing and ordering objects and sorting three-dimensional shapes.

When buying and selling, children will be practising their use of number, as well as familiarising themselves with coins. The class shop could adopt themes, becoming in turn a clothes shop, hat shop, supermarket, chemist, café, toy shop, jeweller's, card shop, post office, newsagent or whatever is required. Use the home corner to assist with such activities.

Morning snacks

If children are allowed to bring their own snacks to school, the food value can sometimes be poor while the salt, sugar and additive intake is likely to be high. Some schools therefore encourage children to contribute to a class fund which is used to provide a range of suitably healthy snacks. When these are given out to children the opportunities for activity and discussion involving number, algebra and measures are numerous.

Dressing and undressing

Use this regular activity to familiarise children with the language of number and measurement, and bring about understanding of the concepts involved. Compare the sizes of different clothes, and talk about the order in which they are taken off or put on; 'I took off my shoes first, then second I took off my dress, then third I took off my tights'.

Essential language

Ordinal numbers, count, correct, belongs to, set, big, bigger, biggest, small, smaller, smallest, tall, taller, tallest, more than, less than, enough, not enough, light, lighter than, heavy, heavier than, balances, about the same as, next to, behind, in front of, between, over, under, on top of, beneath, across, through, up, down, open, closed, full, empty, narrow, wide, fast, faster than, slow, slower than, a long time, late, before, after.

ATs 2AB, 3, 4, 5, 8, 11A, 14.

Classroom equipment

Infant classrooms contain a variety of general apparatus which can engage the children in structured play. The following examples demonstrate how in the course of such play they are using mathematical ideas.

Playmats

These are popular pieces of equipment. When using them, children will be comparing and ordering, using common words to describe position, and giving and understanding instructions for movement. The teacher can ask them to count and order numbers, so that they develop an idea of the conservation of number, use addition and subtraction, make sensible estimates of numbers of objects, and select and use criteria for sorting sets of objects.

Farms

Sets of farm animals are a good resource for sorting. In the course of play or discussion with an adult, farms and farm animals also offer great potential for mathematical activities of various sorts.

Essential language

Numbers to ten, colours, the same colour as, next to, little, wide, narrow, big, biggest, bigger than, small, smallest, smaller than, large, largest, larger than, long, longest, longer than, short, shortest, shorter than, fast, fastest, faster than, slow, slowest, slower than, about the same as, sets of, straight, curved, in front of, behind, across, along, through, forwards, backwards, between, along, how many?

ATs 2AB, 3, 4, 5, 8, 11AB, 12.

Games

Games are a highly popular feature of the school day, especially with younger children, with whom short games are often used to break up the day or to end sessions. The following games, many of which are well known, provide stimulating contexts for developing early ideas of number.

Skittles

This well-known and popular game can be used to involve children in the programme of study for number.

Throwing and counting

Choose a child and ask him or her to throw and catch a bean bag a number of times between one and ten. Another child then has to clap the number of times that the bag was thrown and caught. If they do this correctly they then become the thrower.

In the ring

Ten children are chosen, and each is given a number from one to ten. They then trot around like horses in a circus ring. One of the remaining children is selected as a ringmaster, who calls out any number between one and ten. The horses then stop and the child whose number this is then has to nod his or her head the corresponding number of times.

Ringmasters and horses can be changed at intervals.

What's the time, Mr Wolf?

Mr Wolf stands at a distance from the rest of the group and turns his back on them. As the children move towards the wolf they call, 'What's the time Mr Wolf?'. If the wolf gives them a time, such as eight o'clock, they must jump an equivalent number of times. However, if the wolf answers 'Dinner time!' then the children must rush to a designated safe place. If caught before reaching safety, they have to join the wolf.

Guess the number

Ask a child to whisper a number to you. The child then tells the rest of the group that he has selected a number which they have to guess. Before they start to do so they are allowed one clue from the child who has selected the number. When it is their turn to select a number children should be encouraged to find useful clues which show awareness of number. For example:
● This number comes at the bottom of the clock.
● This number comes between five and nine.
● This is the number of legs on a chair.
● This number is two less than how old I am.

Essential language

Numbers to ten, next, is the same as, as many as, together make, add altogether, in front of, behind, forwards, backwards, more than, less than, too few, correct, enough, not enough, is greater than.

ATs 2A, 4.

Board games and dice

Most children enjoy board games, and many simple games on the market offer mathematical experiences such as recognising the number of spots on a die, or moving a stipulated number of spaces along a number line.

Apart from the games on general release, a number can be obtained from educational suppliers and shops which develop or give practice with particular skills and ideas. These can be a useful resource, providing mathematical experiences while the children are engaged in play.

It is important, however, that the rules of any game used at this stage are easily assimilated and that the actual play is

simple and uncomplicated. Often in seeking variations on fairly standard themes unnecessary complications are introduced.

As an alternative to buying games it is cheaper to produce one's own. In doing so one is able to target a specific aim or set of aims.

Dice can be obtained in a variety of sizes, colours, materials and shapes. These can add variety and interest to activities, and also provide starting points for comparing and sorting activities.

Dice of different shapes can be useful when playing some games, providing experience of a greater range of numbers if so desired. Using dice with spotted faces rather than numerals can assist with estimating small amounts, and they can also give rise to activities copying, continuing and devising repeating patterns. Such dice can also help children to count and to appreciate that the size of a set is represented by the last number in the count.

Essential language

Numbers to ten, add, together make, is the same as.

ATs 2A, 3, 4, 5.

Stories, books and drama

Stories and books can be used either directly or indirectly to involve children in mathematical programmes of study.

Many are old favourites, such as *The Three Little Pigs, Snow White and the Seven Dwarfs, The Three Billy Goats Gruff* and *Goldilocks and the Three Bears*. In these stories, numbers are introduced immediately through their titles. Others, such as *The Gingerbread Man, The Enormous Turnip* and *Chicken Licken*, involve children in counting and comparing. Stories such as these are ideal for mime or drama, either within the classroom or for an audience.

A number of books have been produced which concentrate specifically on elements of a mathematics programme, especially familiarisation with numbers to ten, while the popular *Bronto* books (Longman) are intended as an integral part of a major mathematics series. Each of the books in this series concentrates on a particular theme such as shape, position, comparison of sizes or counting.

Here is a list, by no means exhaustive, of books which either set out to address mathematical ideas or can be put to mathematical use.

Attainment Target 2

123 Lift-the-flap! Rod Campbell (Blackie)
Four Pigs and a Bee Heather Melvill (Dinosaur Publications)
One Bear All Alone Caroline Bucknall (Macmillan)
Circus Numbers Rodney Peppe (Viking Kestrel)
Anno's Counting Book Mitsumasa Anno (The Bodley Head/Macmillan)

1 Hunter Pat Hutchins (The Bodley Head/ Puffin)
Ten, Nine, Eight Molly Bang (Julia MacRae/ Puffin)

Attainment Target 8

Alfie Alligator: How Big? How Tall? How Short? How Small? Judy Hindley/Colin King (Collins)
Titch Pat Hutchins (The Bodley Head/ Puffin)

Attainment Target 10

All Shapes and Sizes Shirley Hughes (Walker Books)
Shapes Jan Pienkowski (Heinemann/Puffin)

Attainment Target 11

Rosie's Walk Pat Hutchins (The Bodley Head/Puffin)
Where's Spot? Eric Hill (Heinemann/Puffin)

More than one attainment target

Lucy and Toms's 123 Shirley Hughes (Gollancz)
123 to the Zoo Eric Carle (Hamish Hamilton)
Down the Road Celia Berridge (*Stepping Stones*, Kingfisher)
Mog and the Baby Judith Kerr (Collins)
Mr Gumpy's Outing John Burningham (Cape/Puffin)
Mr Gumpy's Motor Car John Burningham (Cape/Puffin)

Essential language

Numbers to ten, ordinal numbers, big, bigger, biggest, small, smaller, smallest, square, circle, triangle, under, on top of, beside, inside, up, down.

ATs 2AB, 4, 8, 11AB.

Number rhymes

Rhymes and songs have always been a popular way of familiarising children with numerals and giving them some sense of cardinal amounts. Every teacher has his or her own collection of favourites, such as 'One, two, three, four, five, once I caught a fish alive', 'Buns in the baker's shop', 'Five little ducks', 'Speckled frogs', 'Ten green bottles' and 'Ten in a bed'. A number of books are available which attractively illustrate these and other favourites.

Lesser-known songs and rhymes, sometimes written by teachers themselves, are also useful. See if any colleagues with musical expertise can help.

Here are some examples of less familiar rhymes which are ideally performed with appropriate actions.

'I've ten little fingers
And ten little toes,
I've two round eyes,
Two ears and one nose.'

'One puppy, two puppies, three puppies, four,
Lying down on the kitchen floor,
One miaow, two miaows, three miaows, four,
They chased those kittens out of the door.'

'Carol and Dean and Mark and me
Are going out to Anne's for tea,
While they are all out at play,
Will you put the cups for them on a tray?'

'One green train went chuffing down the track,
One green train came chuffing back,
Two blue trains went chuffing down the track,
Two blue trains came chuffing back,
Three red trains went chuffing down the track,
Three red trains came chuffing back . . .'

'One, two, go to the zoo,
Three, four, leopards roar,
Five, six, chimp's tricks,
Seven, eight, penguins wait,
Nine, ten, lions' den.'

Essential language
Numbers to ten, ordinal numbers.

ATs 2A.

Sharing experiences

When children come together to discuss experiences both in and out of school, there are frequent opportunities to develop ideas about number, measures and shape which will arise quite naturally from statements made by the children. For example:
- It was my sister's birthday yesterday.
- I went to the park last night.
- David is coming round to tea at my house tonight.
- We've just got a new car.

In fact, the children often provide so many opportunities that one has to be highly selective about which to take! It is important not to assume too dominant a role in the session, as this may reduce the voluntary contributions of the children.

Essential language
Numbers, ordinal numbers, shape words, comparative words, today, yesterday, tomorrow.

ATs 2AB, 3, 4, 8, 11AB.

Personal characteristics

Children themselves can become members of sets according to their personal characteristics. Criteria such as the following could be used:
- Colour of eyes.
- Colour of hair.
- Length of hair.
- Which side hair is parted.

Criteria will generally need to restrict the count to ten or under, so dividing the children into boys and girls, for example, will probably be inappropriate.

It will greatly add to the fun if the children themselves form sets by standing within a hoop or an outline drawn on the ground by the teacher. Doing this should also help them make sensible estimates of numbers of objects up to ten.

Once the sets have been created, the children should enjoy the adding and subtracting activities which can follow. Sets such as those with green eyes and those with blue eyes could be joined, or two sets compared. As before, the children will eagerly respond when they actually have to perform such operations themselves. While engaging in activities which aim to develop their understanding of number, number operations and estimation, the children will simultaneously be addressing Science Attainment Target 4, which calls for an appreciation of the variation between human beings.

Essential language
Belongs to, colours, is the same colour as, set, sets of, as many as, more, more than, less, less than, few, fewer than, is greater than, together make, add, altogether, tall, short, take away, left with.

ATs 1AB, 2AB, 3, 4, 8, 12.

Clothes

Looking at what children wear will provide numerous opportunities for:
- sorting and setting objects,
- counting,
- adding and subtracting,
- estimating,
- continuing and devising repeating patterns,
- comparing and ordering.

There are many opportunities for these activities, with either the whole class or a particular group. Depending on whether school uniform is worn, children may have to base their discussion on what is worn out of school in order to have the relevant information.

Consider such questions as:
- How many children have a dress which is the same colour as Stephanie's?
- How many buttons do you have on your clothes?
- How many different sorts of trousers are being worn today? (Or if uniform is worn, how many different sorts do the children have at home?)
- Whose clothes have the greatest number of different colours?

These are just a few possibilities, each of which offers potential for addressing statements of attainment within a number of targets.

Essential language
Colours, the same colour as, match, find its partner, set, sets of, more than, less than, fewer than, big, bigger than, biggest, small, smaller than, smallest, long, longer than, longest, wide, wider than, widest, over, up, down.

ATs 1AB, 2AB, 3, 4, 5, 8, 9ABC, 12, 13AB.

PE

PE sessions provide a number of opportunities for developing children's knowledge and understanding of position. In the course of such sessions, the advice and instructions given by the teacher contain many examples of positional language, such as, 'Can you climb over that form?' or, 'Why don't you try going under the bench?'

This sort of activity has been part of PE sessions with young children for many years, and within the National Curriculum it can consciously be used for delivering Attainment Target 11 at Level 1. It may be that teachers will want to concentrate on certain aspects of position in space within particular sessions, when children are engaged in activity on the floor and on apparatus.

When planning apparatus layouts, position the pieces of equipment to offer maximum opportunities for children to perform a wide range of actions within the space they occupy. The examples below can work with six groups of children.
• Provide a set of mats, preferably small ones, set out at irregular intervals and giving opportunities for moving forwards or backwards, around, between, across or from one to the other.
• Provide a set of forms for children to travel along, moving forwards or backwards, over, under or through.

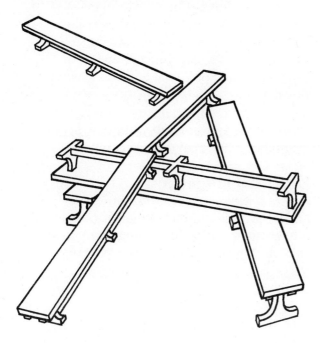

• Children can climb up a ramp made from a bench hooked onto a stand. They then jump down, perhaps turning or twisting in the air to land pointing forwards or backwards.
• Make an arrangement of metal frames and benches, placing some of the benches as ramps and others as bridges. This provides opportunities for movements forwards and backwards, on top, off, over, under, along, up, down and through the apparatus.
• Use wall bars for the children to clamber through, between, in and out of, moving up and down and from side to side.
• Have a small box which can be used for jumping on to or off, and for climbing over.

Essential language
Forwards, backwards, to the side, turn, around, between, across, along, over, under, through, up, down, on top, in, out, on, off.

ATs 11AB.

Floor turtles

The floor turtle is an ideal means of delivering the part of the programme of study at this level which relates to position in space.

Floor turtles come in a variety of guises. Some are attached via a lead to the keyboard of the computer, and others receive instructions via beams of infra-red light. In order to move, all turtles are dependent upon instructions being given to the computer. The keys when pressed move the turtle left, right, forwards and backwards when accompanied by a number. For example:
↑ 500 return
will propel the turtle forward 500 units, while the instruction
↓ 250 return
will send it halfway back to the start. The unit of rotation is degrees, so
→ 90 return
will turn the turtle 90° or one right angle to the right, and
← 180 return
will turn the turtle through 180° or two

right angles so that it faces in the opposite direction from the starting point.

To simplify this routine for the children, and to avoid them having to use what to them are unrealistically large numbers, a 'concept keyboard' can be used. The children can then be presented with a limited number of options determined by the teacher when preparing the concept keyboard overlay. This can make the exercise simpler and less alarming for the children.

To add fun to activities involving floor turtles, many schools decorate them to resemble a variety of creatures, often characters in maths or reading schemes used within the school.

Essential language
Forwards, backwards, turn, left, right, between, along, through, over, under.

ATs 11AB.

How many pips?

Just how many pips does an apple have, and do all apples contain the same number? There will be no shortage of volunteers to attempt answers to this sort of question, particularly when investigators have the opportunity to eat their experiments!

A number of contexts exist for this activity: the topic of 'Harvest', a discussion of 'things we like to eat', or even just lunchtime! In tackling such an investigation the children will have opportunities to engage in all elements of the programme of study for number. In addition they will be able to record the results of their investigations with real

objects and drawings, and create simple mapping diagrams showing relationships.

Teachers will think of a number of variations on this theme, some of them seasonal. For example:
- How many peas in a pod?
- How many seeds in a bean?
- How many pips in an orange?

Essential language
Numbers to ten, more, more than, less, less than, few, fewer than.

ATs 1ABC, 2AB, 3, 4, 8, 13AB.

On the road

When groups of children have to go out of school, either walking along pavements or travelling by coach, use the opportunity to refer to safety considerations. Use comparative language, such as taller than, bigger than, longer than, faster than.

In the course of such activities children will develop ideas about the size, speed and volume of traffic and will therefore learn about the potential hazards which it presents.

You may be able to observe the traffic from some vantage point within the school grounds, rather than venturing out.

Essential language
Colours, the same colour as, little, big, small, large, larger than, smaller than, long, longer than, short, shorter than, tall, taller than, in front of, behind, heavy, fast, faster than, slow, slower than, quick, quicker than.

ATs 1BC, 8.

Sorting

The links between science and mathematics are recognised and referred to in the non-statutory advice provided by the National Curriculum Council.

As part of their science programme of study at Level 1 the children have to describe objects in terms of simple properties such as shape, colour and texture. This requires them to select criteria for sorting a set of objects, and to apply the criteria consistently.

It is useful in activities of this kind to have available a variety of collections of objects. Ideally each collection should contain as many different materials as possible, and be restricted to ten items or less, which would then provide opportunities for addressing Attainment Targets 3 and 4.

An additional fillip can be provided to this activity if the children can make a game out of partitioning. A child is chosen and asked to partition a collection of objects into sets using her own criteria. When this has been done the other children can suggest which criteria were employed. The first to guess correctly can then partition the next set.

Essential language
Colours, is the same colour as, belongs to, is the same as, set, sets of, as many as, more than, less than, fewer than, big, bigger than, small, smaller than, short, shorter than, wide, wider than, large, larger than, narrow, narrower than, fat, fatter than, thin, thinner than, light, lighter than, heavy, heavier than, holds more than, holds less than, straight, curved, flat, cube, cuboid, cylinder, square, rectangle, round, circle, triangle.

ATs 3, 4, 10A, 12, 13AB.

Shape pictures

Shaped pieces can be arranged to construct a variety of pictures.

This type of activity can be presented in a number of ways:
- Finding the various shapes within pictures given to the children.
- Sticking the appropriate pre-cut shapes on to a prepared outline.
- Using pre-cut paper or plastic shapes to construct pictures of the children's own design.
- Letting the children make their own shapes by drawing around templates and cutting them out, then using these to design pictures of their own.

Essential language
Square, rectangle, circle, triangle, next to, colours, is the same colour as, big, tall, short, small, narrow, thick, thin, wide, about the same as, between, above, below, over, under, on top of.

ATs 2AB, 3, 5, 10AB.

Greetings cards

Young children love bringing birthday cards to school for their friends to see. Use this as a context for reading, writing and ordering numbers – although as the ages within one class are not likely to span a wide range of numbers, children from other classes could be invited in when convenient. Try to avoid possible embarrassment to those children who may not have as many cards as the others.

Children also make cards for a variety of celebrations, events and festivals. The children could use repeat patterns or two-dimensional shapes when designing their cards.

Essential language
Numbers, the same as.

ATs 2A, 5, 10B.

Number fun

Here are three simple activities which give children experience of the parts of the mathematics programme of study relating to number.

Funnyuns

What you need
Some cut-out animal footprints as shown, paper, paints, colour pencils.

What to do
Give the children a cut-out footprint each. Written on the footprint are instructions about the appearance of some imaginary animals, which the children have to follow in drawing the creatures; for example, 'two heads, six legs', or 'three legs, five tails'.

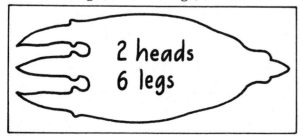

2 heads
6 legs

Addimals

What you need
A large picture of an animal, a small object to use as a token.

What to do
Draw or place a large picture of an animal on the floor. Divide the body into numbered areas. Select a small object and give it a number value such as 42, so that when children toss it on to the animal this number has to be added to the number inside the section in which the object landed.

Cubies

What you need
Squared paper, coloured cubes.

What to do
Draw some animal shapes on the squared paper, and let the children make the creatures by filling the squares with cubes. First, however, they have to estimate or count how many they will need and take

the right number of cubes from the pile provided.

Essential language
Numbers to ten, big, long, tall, short, fat, thin, large, small, too many, too few, enough, not enough, more, more than, together make, less, less than, add, count, altogether, collect.

ATs 2AB, 3, 4.

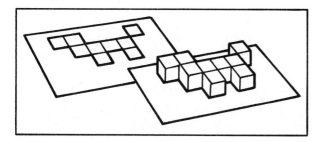

Search and find

This activity can help children compare and make estimates about objects in terms of size, shape and position.

What you need
A collection of about ten everyday objects.

What to do
Place an assortment of objects in front of the children. Ask one of the children to choose an item and whisper its name to you. The other children then take turns to guess which object was chosen. Each time a guess is offered, a clue must be given which refers to the size, shape or position of the mystery object in relation to the others. For example:
- it is taller,
- it is heavier,
- it is in front,
- it isn't a round shape.

The child who guesses correctly then takes a turn to select an object. A number of variations on this basic idea could be used, perhaps involving the children in moving around the room following directions given to help them search. The variety of objects could be restricted in order to concentrate attention more exclusively, or the type of clues which can be given could be restricted, for instance by referring to size only.

Essential language
Numbers to ten, colours, curved, round, in front of, behind, next to, flat, bigger than, shorter than, wider than, narrower than, fatter than, thinner than, larger than, fuller than, holds more than, holds less than, cube, cylinder, cuboid, square, rectangle, triangle, circle.

ATs 8, 10A, 11A.

Tube families

This is an activity which children will enjoy, and which will give them opportunities to sort and compare a range of three-dimensional objects.

What you need
Plastic and cardboard containers of various shapes and sizes, plain and coloured paper, adhesive, sticky tape, paints, coloured pencils, sand or beans for filling containers.

What to do
Wrap wide strips of paper around a selection of plastic drinks bottles, washing-up liquid bottles, drink cans, cardboard tubes, and so on.

The children can then help to make characters out of them by drawing, sticking on or colouring in the features and clothes. The different containers will provide a variety of sizes, and children can group them in families.

When made, the characters can be played with or displayed. In either case there will be many opportunities to compare and order them in terms of size.

In addition, by filling or part-filling some of the tubes, bottles or cans, the characters can be compared and ordered on the basis of their different weights.

Although tubes and cylinders are probably best for this activity, other three-dimensional shapes can be used to familiarise children with different shapes and their names. 'Families' in a variety of shapes would make a valuable resource for sorting.

Essential language
Big, bigger than, biggest, large, larger than, largest, small, smaller than, smallest, short, shorter than, shortest, tall, taller than, tallest, fat, fatter than, fattest, thin, thinner than, thinnest, heavy, heavier than, heaviest, light, lighter than, lightest, cube, cuboid, circle, cylinder, tube, rectangle, square, in front of, behind, next to.

ATs 1AB, 2A, 4, 5, 8, 9AB, 10B, 11A.

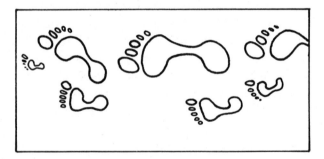

Hands and feet

For teachers who are brave enough, making hand and foot prints is bound to be popular with the children. In fact, with adequate supervision, it does not have to be as daunting as it may sound. Making prints is a good art activity, and it can also lead to experiments comparing the texture of different paints. The foot or hand prints can also be compared in terms of length and width.

What you need
Large sheets of paper or a roll of wallpaper, trays of paint, soapy water and towels, another adult to help supervise.

What to do
If you have a roll of wallpaper you could let the children make a trail along it. In doing so they could devise or follow a repeat pattern such as red, green, red, green, and so on.

When dry, the prints could be used as a number line, and the children could be given instructions for moving along it, for example, 'Move forward three steps', or 'Move backwards six steps'. A number line consisting of eleven prints numbered from nought to ten would allow children to perform addition and subtraction operations moving along the line.

Essential language
Numbers to ten, ordinal numbers, colours, forwards, backwards, along, start, together make, add, count, count on.

ATs 2A, 4, 5, 8, 11B.

Boats

Boats with numbers are a popular and much-used piece of apparatus with children at this level. In addition to using boats obtained through educational suppliers, the children could be involved in making their own. Even better if these boats can actually float!

Such an activity will obviously require plenty of adult support and supervision, but the range of cross-curricular statements which it addresses should make it worthwhile.

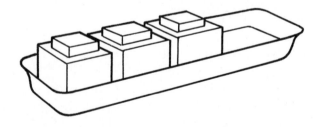

What you need
A range of junk material such as plastic pots, foil trays, lolly sticks and paper; some small objects such as construction cubes and small toys to be passengers; adhesive, sticky tape, scissors.

What to do

Ask the children to make little boats from the junk material, and encourage them to think carefully about their designs. During the design and planning stage of the project decisions have to be made, many of them demanding the use and application of mathematics.

● Who or what are the passengers going to be? Try cubes, LEGO figures, and so on.
● From what materials can the boats be made?
● What shape should they be?
● What size will they need to be to carry one passenger, two passengers, three passengers . . .?

Children should have fun making their boats, while addressing the appropriate statement of Design and Technology Attainment Target 3.

When completed the boats can be tested, and this can also involve using mathematical language and techniques.

Essential language

Numbers to ten, is the same as, together make, add, take away, leaves, too many, too few, not enough.

ATs 2A, 3, 8, 10B.

Trains

Model trains are a popular piece of play equipment in many classrooms, along with their track layouts, which the children can arrange for themselves. When the carriages are attached, the language of ordinal number can be used – first carriage, second carriage, third carriage, and so on.

Drawings and paintings of trains and their carriages can also be used to develop a knowledge and understanding of ordinal numbers.

What you need

A large picture of a train with a number of carriages labelled '1st', '2nd', '3rd', etc. The carriages should not be stuck down at the top, so they form pockets. You also need some card cut-outs for passengers, or paper and paints for the children to make their own.

What to do

Give the children instructions for how many passengers to put in each carriage; for example, 'Put two passengers in the second carriage, and four passengers in the third carriage.'

When the carriages have been filled, ask questions such as, 'How many passengers are on the train?' or 'How many more passengers are in the third carriage than the second?'

Essential language

Numbers to ten, ordinal numbers, next to, more than, less than, fewer than, holds more, holds less, together make, is as many as, add, count, altogether, behind, in front of.

ATs 2A, 3, 4, 5.

Postman's bag

This activity helps to counter any erroneous notions that mass is necessarily a result of the size of an object. Colourful wrapping paper will add to the appeal of the activity, and children will enjoy having the chance to be a postman!

What you need
Containers and packets of various shapes and sizes, which are filled or part-filled with sand or beans, and then wrapped in wrapping paper.

What to do
Make a collection of parcels which differ in shape, size and mass. Ensure that there is no relationship between the size and mass of the parcels; ie that the largest ones are not always heaviest.

Then put the parcels into a 'postman's bag', and choose a postman to deliver pairs of parcels to some of the other children. When children receive a pair of parcels they must compare them, deciding which is heavier and which lighter. Their estimates could then be checked using a bucket balance.

The children can take turns to be the postman, and the activity can be extended by asking the postman to deliver three parcels which then have to be put in weight order by the recipient.

'Postman' games using these parcels can then be encouraged in the home corner.

Essential language
Heavy, heavier than, heaviest, light, lighter than, lightest, about the same as, balances, level.

ATs 8, 10A, 11A.

30

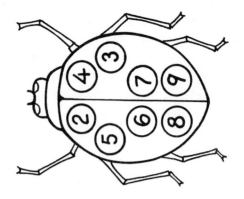

Ladybird spots

This simple game will give children opportunities to add or subtract numbers to get an answer of ten or under.

What you need
'Ladybird' boards as shown, coloured counters, dice or cubes whose sides are numbered from one to four.

What to do
This is a game for two players, who each have a pool of counters. They each take half of the ladybird and attempt to put counters on the spots on their side of the creature.

The players take turns to roll the die and take the appropriate number of counters from their pool. Then they add to or take from this number the number required to bring the total up to that indicated on any one of the ladybird's spots. If a player calculates this correctly, he or she can place a counter on the spot. The aim is to fill all the spots.

Essential language
Numbers to ten, together make, the same as, add, take away, leaves.

ATs 2AB, 3.

Estimation games

Games such as the following three will encourage children to make estimates of numbers up to ten, and lead to some appreciation of the conservation of number. In order to play these games the children will need a pack of cards prepared by the teacher. Each card displays a different number of familiar objects, such as bottles, cups, socks, buttons etc.

To assist the teacher in this task, rubber stamps are available which can be used to print pictures onto the cards. The pictures should be printed or drawn in a variety of configurations rather than in the conventional arrangements commonly used on playing cards. This will ensure that when making estimates children will not be relying on identifying patterns. If using ready-made packs of cards, check that the children cannot rely too heavily on patterns, arrangements and shape. Using such clues will develop an understanding of number, but will not give practice in estimation.

Guess the number
This game can be played by any number of players.

What you need
A pack of cards showing groups of objects in several different configurations, as described above.

What to do
Place the cards in a stack face downwards in front of one of the children, who then has to estimate (not count) the number of items on the card. If the estimate is correct, the player keeps the card. If incorrect, the card has to be returned to the bottom of the pack. The pack is passed to each of the children in turn, and play continues in this way until all of the cards in the pack have been acquired by the players.

Snap
This popular game can be played by two to four players.

What you need
A pack of cards showing groups of objects.

What to do
The children take turns to flip over a card, and they shout 'SNAP!' if they think that the number of items on the last card to be turned over is the same as that on the previous card. Whoever is first to shout 'SNAP!' keeps the pile of discarded cards, and play continues until someone has won all the cards.

Pelmanism
This is also a well-known and much-played game which can be played by a number of children.

What you need
A pack of cards showing groups of objects.

What to do
Spread out the cards and place them face down. The children then turn over any two of the cards, taking care to put them back in their original position. If the number of items on each card is the same, then the player turning them over retains the cards. If not, then the cards are turned back again, once more taking care to keep them in the same position, and the next child has a turn.

Essential language
Numbers to ten, the same as, more, more than, too many, less, less than, few, fewer than, too few, not enough.

ATs 1C, 2AB, 4.

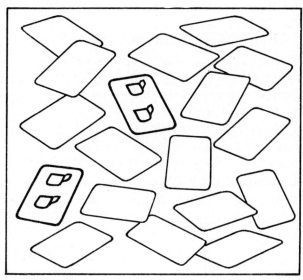

Walking to school

This game for up to four players gives practice in the addition of numbers up to ten.

What you need
Copies of the board, as illustrated, two dice numbered one to four (with two faces blank), a counter or token for each player.

What to do
Each player starts at one of the houses at the corners of the board, and places a token on their house. The players then take turns to shake the dice. The total of the two uppermost faces represents the number of steps which can be taken along the pavement on the board: for example, a two and a four would enable a player to move their token six spaces forward, while a one and a blank would allow a move of one space only.

Players must stop before they cross the road, and wait until they throw a blank, even if this means that they cannot use all of their 'steps'.

The first person to reach school is the winner.

Essential language
Numbers to ten, the same as, more, more than, too many, less, less than, few, fewer than, too few, not enough.

ATs 2A, 3, 4.

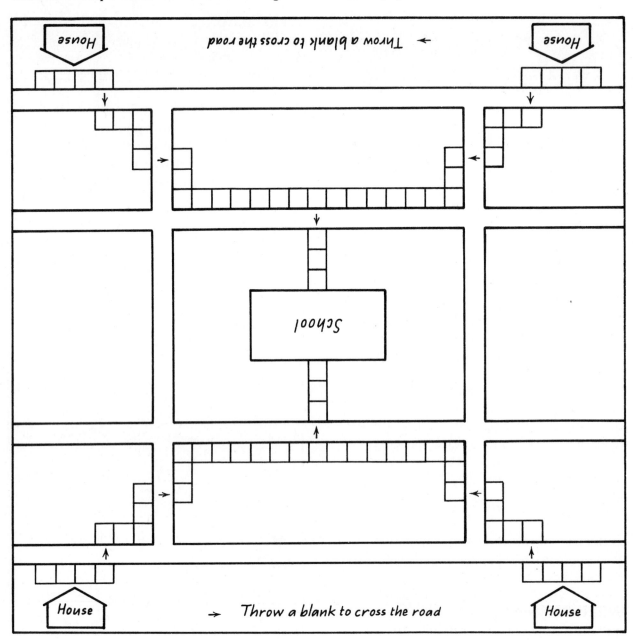

Level 1 glossary of terms

The following glossary explains some of the mathematical terms which are contained within the statements of attainment for mathematics at Level 1.

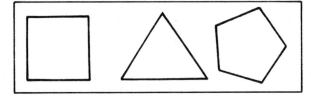

Two-dimensional shapes
Shapes which possess only the two dimensions of length and breadth, but not depth; for example, squares, triangles and pentagons.

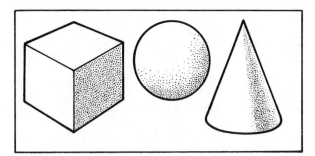

Three-dimensional shapes
Shapes which possess the dimensions of length, breadth and depth, otherwise known as solid shapes; for example, cubes, spheres and cones.

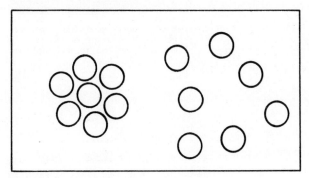

Conservation of number
When a set of objects is arranged differently, the number of objects remains the same.

Estimation
Making sensible judgements of quantities without measuring.

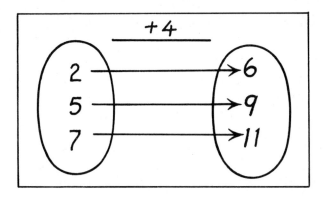

Mapping diagram
A diagram which shows the relationship or correspondence between two or more sets, the corresponding members of each set being joined by means of arrows.

Possible outcomes
The different results possible with a random event. For example, when tossing a coin there are two possible outcomes: heads or tails.

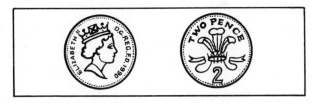

Random events
Events which occur in no set sequence or defined pattern.

Set
A group of objects which belong together; for example, cabbages, beans and peas belong to the set of vegetables. Each object in a set is called a 'member' or an 'element'.

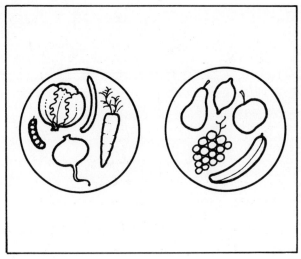

Level 1: Programme of Study

This diagram shows how the programme of study can be expanded, suggesting teaching stages where applicable.

- Match by one-to-one correspondence.
- Sort into sets and subsets; sort by partitioning.
- Match to find equivalent and non-equivalent sets.
- Pictorial representation and semi-tallying.
- Counting.
- Match a number symbol to a set.
- Recognise, read and write number words.
- Order non-equivalent sets.
- Order cardinal numbers.

Using and applying mathematics
- Use materials for a practical task.
- Talk about own work and ask questions.
- Make predictions based on experience.

Number
- Count, read, write and order numbers to at least ten.
- Understand conservation of number.
- Use addition and subtraction with numbers no greater than ten, in the context of real objects.
- Make a sensible estimation of a number of objects up to ten.

Algebra
- Copy, continue and devise repeating patterns.

Measures
- Compare and order objects without measuring; use appropriate language.

Shape and space
- Sort and classify two- and three-dimensional shapes.
- Build three-dimensional solid shapes and draw two-dimensional shapes and describe them.
- Use common words to describe a position.
- Give and understand instructions for movement along a line.

Handling data
- Select criteria for sorting a set of objects, and apply them consistently.
- Record with objects or by drawing.
- Create simple mapping diagrams showing relationships, and interpret them.
- Recognise possible outcomes of random events.

- Understand the composition of numbers from one to ten.
- Record simple additions by mapping.
- Number bonds.
- Count on.
- Use the + symbol in vertical addition.
- Find the difference by matching and counting.
- Count back.
- Take away.
- Use the − symbol in vertical subtraction.

- Copy sequential patterns where colour, shape or size are alternated.
- Recognise and complete sequential patterns with three or more elements.
- Construct sequential patterns.
- Make simple patterns using single digits.

- Early play experiences.
- Use descriptive language.
- Find a set of objects of about the same length or mass.
- Estimate the capacity of an object by matching and balancing.
- Compare sets of three or more items.
- Order objects by matching, balancing and estimation.

- Have an awareness of shape and shape vocabulary.
- Make sets of two- and three-dimensional objects according to shape.
- Partition sets of two- and three-dimensional shapes by different criteria.

- Use simple given criteria to sort a collection.
- Partition sets into sub-sets using given criteria.
- Adopt individual criteria for sorting objects into sets.
- Adopt individual criteria for dividing a set into sub-sets.

Level 1 : attainment targets 1–14

Use this chart to check which attainment targets are covered by each activity.

ACTIVITY	1 A	1 B	1 C	2 A	2 B	3	4	5	8	9 A	9 B	9 C	10 A	10 B	11 A	11 B	12	13 A	13 B	14
Classroom situations				●	●	●	●	●	●						●					●
Classroom equipment				●	●	●	●	●	●						●	●	●			
Games				●			●													
Board games and dice				●		▲	●	●												
Stories, books and drama				●	●		●		●						●	●				
Number rhymes				▲																
Sharing experiences				●	●	●	●		●						●	●				●
Personal characteristics	●	●		●	●	●	●		●						●					
Clothes	●	●		●	●	●	●	●	●	●	●	●				●	●	●		
PE															▲	▲				
Floor turtles															●	▲				
How many pips?	▲	▲	▲	●	●	●	●		●											
On the road		●	▲						▲											
Sorting						▲	▲						●				●	●	●	
Shape pictures				●	●	●		●					●	▲						
Greetings cards				▲				●						●						
Number fun				●	●	●	●													
Search and find									▲				●		●					
Tube families	●	●		●			●	●	▲	●	●			●	●					
Hands and feet				●			●	▲	●							▲				
Boats				▲		●			●					●						
Trains				▲		●	●	●												
Postman's bag									▲				●		●					
Ladybird spots				●	●	▲														
Estimation games			●	●	●			●												
Walking to school				●			●	●												

Key: ● = touches on
▲ = especially
relevant

Level 1 : Contexts

This chart shows the wider contexts of each activity.

ACTIVITY	Everyday situations	Everyday problems	Games and fun	Maths problems	Maths investigations	Calculator activities	Computer activities	English (Core)	Science (Core)	Art (Foundation)	PE (Foundation)	History (Foundation)	Geography (Foundation)	Music (Foundation)	Technology (Foundation)	Local Curriculum	RE	Possible topic link	School-wide themes
Classroom situations	•	•	•					•			•					•		•	•
Classroom equipment	•		•					•											
Games			•					•			•								
Board games and dice			•	•															
Stories, books and drama								•										•	•
Number rhymes			•					•						•					
Sharing experiences	•	•						•								•			
Personal characteristics									•		•					•			•
Clothes	•							•											•
P E			•								•								
Floor turtles			•				•												
How many pips?				•				•										•	•
On the road												•				•			•
Sorting				•				•											
Shape pictures										•									
Greetings cards	•		•					•									•	•	
Number fun			•	•				•											
Search and find			•	•															
Tube families			•						•										
Hands and feet			•						•	•								•	•
Boats									•					•					•
Trains				•					•										•
Postman's bag			•																
Ladybird spots			•																
Estimation games			•																
Walking to school	•	•	•									•							•

36

Chapter two
Level 2

Introduction

Children at Level 2 can begin to apply mathematics to a wide range of situations. At this stage they are becoming increasingly aware of the immediate world around them and the ways in which they can influence it. A great deal of interesting work can result from their tackling a specific problem. This can involve them in devising rotas, compiling graphs and charts, working out the most efficient way of using resources, and sorting and classifying different types of information.

The situations and problems to which children are asked to apply mathematics at this stage should be quite straightforward and unitary. Make sure, when playing mathematical games, that the children understand the rules and know what is expected of them. Games are a good way of showing children that mathematics can be interesting, relevant and exciting, but it is also important to make sure that children have enough time to talk through the new ideas they are encountering and discuss anything which puzzles them.

School meals

There is plenty of scope for involving the children in the organisation of the daily school meal and midday break. Besides increasing children's knowledge of health and diet, this can involve the use of many mathematical skills. Here are some activities in which you may like to involve the children.

School dinners
The children will need a list showing who usually stays for school dinner, who stays for sandwiches and who goes home. Tell them how many children are present on that particular day. From this they can work out the numbers who are absent, and then the numbers who are staying for school dinner and for sandwiches.

Milk time
Some schools distribute milk at break-time, particularly in the infant department. If this is the case the children can be involved in calculating the numbers who require milk and counting out and delivering the milk, if it is safe for them to do this.

A check can be made on the amount of milk drunk each day. Comparisons need to be made first of all between a school milk bottle (one third of a pint) and a pint bottle, then by using a diagram to group the small bottles in threes, it is possible to see the number of pints of milk that the class drinks.

40

Diet surveys

By collecting information from their own class and other classes the children can look at:

- The selection of food on offer.
- The most popular choice of food for that day.
- Whether vegetarian or other dietary requirements are catered for.
- Whether any changes could be made to achieve a balanced diet.

The children would need to carry out surveys, tabulate and graph their results, and consider how the graphs would change if their recommendations were put into practice.

Other activities could involve the timing and distribution of the meal, the table arrangements and the organisation of a rota system for the classes.

Essential language

Numbers, half, third, all, survey, graph.

ATs 1ABC, 3AB, 12AB, 13AB.

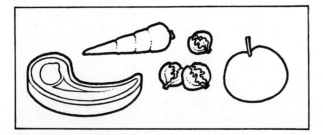

Break-times

Break-times in most schools present various situations which may give rise to difficulties; collecting coats and going outside, playing in the playground, ensuring playground safety, and so on. Attempting a solution to some of the problems which may arise can involve mathematical work.

Going outside

Ask a small group of children to study the procedure for going outside at break-times. Discuss the reasons for such a study; it is in the interests of safety. If there is more than one exit to the playground they could count and compare the number of children using the various exits. They could devise a way of timing how long it takes everyone

to go outside. They could also look at the size of the groups that form as the children walk out of school. This may lead to a list of recommendations to be put into practice.

Playground games

A survey could be conducted into the number of children who play games, and the number who stand around. The children could make a list of the games which are played, and suggest ways of including those who are not involved.

Maybe the children could devise games of their own? This may lead to a request for more lines to be painted on the playground – a project which needs to be worked out properly. Can the children suggest ways to do this? How can they make sure the lines will fit?

The children may have quite a few ideas for games to play. These need to be carefully selected and introduced, to familiarise all the children with the rules so that as many as possible will join in. Too many markings painted on the playground may confuse them. Possible games might be a variation on hopscotch, or a game using a large wiggly number line which has spaces for the children to step into, and possibly a large die.

Wet playtimes

These can also be a problem. The children need some form of relaxation and an opportunity to detach themselves from their class-work.

Ask the children to make a list of things they can do to occupy themselves during wet playtimes.

Which activities on the list are the most popular? Can they suggest a way of organising the activities so that everyone gets their turn? (Do they need to keep a record? How can this be done?)

Can the children devise a way of storing any equipment required so that it is readily accessible?

Essential language

Numbers, ordinal numbers, seconds, minutes, list.

ATs 1ABC, 2A, 8AC, 9AC.

At the shop

There are plenty of opportunities for practising shopping activities using the class shop. The activities need to be structured and planned so that they are built up gradually.

First, the teacher can act as shopkeeper with a small group of children. Items can be bought, and a record made of the amount spent and the change given. Get the children to talk the transaction through; 'I have 10p, I am going to buy a pencil for 6p so I will have 4p change.' The children can be asked to take a certain sum to the shop and to work out what items they can buy for that amount, or to work out the change they will get from 30p if they buy two items costing 12p and 8p.

Essential language

Spend, cost, pay, buy, coin, pence, the same as, more than, less than, change, right amount.

ATs 2A, 3ABC, 8B.

Looking after living things

Children should be aware of the needs of other living organisms, and they should be given the opportunity to take care of them. At the same time this provides a context for the development of many mathematical skills such as measuring and handling data and number.

Plants

● Conduct an investigation into the conditions for growth, monitoring and recording the growth of various plants under different conditions over a period of time.
● Monitor the plants' growth on a block graph. Discuss the graph with the children, and ask what differences there would be if the plants were not watered.
● Try to find out which places in the room are best for the plants, noting the changes to the plants when they are moved. Can the children suggest possible causes?
● Investigate how often the plants need to be watered, and how much water to give

them. Monitor and record this, and compare the amount given to different types of plants. Note the effect of seasonal changes on the plants.
● Devise a classroom rota for looking after the plants.

Pets

● Monitor and record the growth of classroom pets over a period of time.
● Measure and record the amount of food and water they need each day.
● Investigate the animals' food preferences.
● Record the amount of sleep they need.
● Look at any variations in their activities at different times of the day.
● Devise a classroom rota for looking after the pets.

Birds

● Make a bird cake. The normal ingredients for bird cake are seeds, nuts, raisins, fat, bacon rind and breadcrumbs – but you can vary the proportions used and see if the birds show any preference.
● Over a period of time, monitor how much has been eaten and how frequently the food is visited.

Essential language

Numbers, millimetres, centimetres, block graph, rota, seconds, minutes, hours.

ATs 1ABC, 2A, 3A, 8AC, 9ABC, 12AB, 13A.

Time

The following activity addresses Attainment Target 8, and helps children recognise the need to use a standard measure to record time.

Various instruments can be made to record the passing of time, for example sand timers and rocker timers.

A candle clock can also be made, with pins stuck in the side at regular intervals, so that as the candle burns the pins fall away.

Timing activities

A number of children can perform the same activity with a selection of different timers set in action at the same moment. Try timing these activities:
- Threading beads.
- Building towers four cubes high.
- Writing the number five as many times as possible.
- Drawing triangles.
- Hopping.
- Bouncing balls.

The results can be recorded, graphed, analysed and compared, which will lead to an appreciation of the need to use a standard unit to record and measure time, and the reason for the introduction of the clock and hours, minutes and seconds. The activities can then be tried once more, timed by a clock.

Essential language

Sand timer, rocker timer, candle clock, start, begin, stop, finish, time, faster than, slower than, how many, block graph, measure, seconds, minutes, hours.

ATs 2A, 3AB, 8AC.

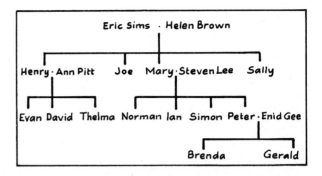

Past times

The past can often be fascinating, and it can be relevant to many different topics; the life of a tree, the history of the local area, a study of family trees, or any project on transport, housing, clothes, food, industry and so on – the list is endless.

The past does not have to be distant. Children have a direct link with the past through their parents and grandparents, who are a valuable source of information. They could talk to their older relatives about the changes they have seen, and the findings could be collated, graphed and compared with the present day.

Here are some possible topics for investigation:
- Methods of getting to school.
- Popular playground games.
- Number of children in the family.
- Popular pastimes.
- Popular toys and what they are made from.
- Methods of heating and lighting the house.

Essential language

Numbers, data, findings, graph, compare.

ATs 1ABC, 2A, 9AB, 12AB, 13AB.

Seeds and fruit

A study of seeds and fruit brings in many mathematical skills and concepts. It also links in well with other areas of the curriculum. Whilst providing children with an opportunity to sort, classify, measure and estimate, the project also allows them to collect, process and interpret data. A look at fruit will also help children to see its nutritional value, and increase knowledge about healthy eating habits.

The best way of starting is to take the children for a walk outside to collect seeds and fruits. The practicability of this does depend on accessibility and the time of year. Alternatively, fruit and·seeds can be brought into school by you or by the children.

Tree fruits include acorns, conkers, beech nuts and sycamore seeds. Plant fruits include lupin (seeds in a pod), dandelion (parachute-like seeds), poppy (its seeds are encased in a pod which acts like a pepperpot), blackberry and elderberry (seeds encased in juicy or colourful fruit). A variety of edible fruits such as apples, oranges and pears could be brought in as well.

Sort the seeds and fruit out into those which are edible and those which are inedible.

Inedible fruits

Taking the non-edible fruits first, ask the children to sort them out according to any criteria they can think of, such as size, colour, shape and thickness of skin. The children's findings can be shown in graphs.

Dispersal
Take a seed-pod or fruit apart – what does it contain? Is there just one seed? Is it possible to estimate and count the number of seeds?

Discuss seed dispersal – what is it, and why does it take place? Can the children suggest how seeds might be dispersed? Can they classify the seeds according to the method of dispersal?

Edible fruits

Next look at edible fruits; make sure that the children wash their hands first. Collect a variety of fruit, and again sort and classify them on the basis of criteria selected by the children. How many edible fruits can they name? Remember that some vegetables are actually fruits (for example tomatoes).

Weight
Estimate the weight of the fruit by handling and comparing it with other objects around the classroom, then check the weight using a balance.

Make a set of objects which are lighter or heavier than an orange. Estimate and discover, using a balance, objects which weigh the same as a melon.

Order three types of fruit according to their weight by handling. Then compare the weight of pieces of fruit using arbitrary measures. Record the results on a pictogram. Discuss with the children the need for standard measures.

In order to give the children experience of the conservation of weight, select two similar sized oranges and place them on a balance to show they weigh the same. Then subdivide one into halves or quarters. Check the weight on the balance again.

Next, introduce the kilogram, and sort and classify the fruit into groups lighter and heavier than a kilogram. Then try making groups of things lighter and heavier than half a kilogram.

Constancy

Compare several fruits of the same type, for example apples, to see if they have the same number of pips. In groups, the children could work on a variety of investigations to explore the constancy in such things as the number of pips in a pear, or the amount of peel on an apple (if you can manage to cut the peel off in one go!). They could also compare the number of pips in an orange with the number of pips in a pear, an apple and a melon.

When cutting up the fruit, discuss fractions – how many halves and how many quarters make a whole one? How many quarters make a half?

Time can also be spent in estimating numbers. Estimate the number of apples in a bag, the number of oranges in a box, the number of pears on a tray, and so on.

Fruit surveys

The children can carry out surveys to find the most popular fruit. Now that more unusual fruits are available you could have a fruit tasting session to discover which is the most popular.

Using a world map, map out the fruits according to their country of origin. By linking the places of origin to your town with string, compare the distances the fruit has travelled.

Bring in some tinned fruit in similar sized tins, and work out the best buy in terms of quantity. Drain off the juice and measure and weigh the fruit to compare contents. Tinned fruit with sugar added can be tasted and the taste compared to that with no added sugar.

Make a fruit salad for the whole class. Get the children to work out how much is required for everyone.

Weigh a handful of dried peas, soak them in water overnight, then discuss what has happened to them. How might the peas have increased in size, and how can we find this out? Should we have measured the amount of water before and after, too?

Many more possibilities still exist, and practically all of the ones listed above satisfy the attainment targets for handling data in one way or another.

Essential language

Numbers, colours, large, larger, largest, small, smaller, smallest, gram, kilogram, light, lighter, lightest, heavy, heavier, heaviest, pictogram, graph, half, quarter, estimate, survey.

ATs 1ABC, 2AB, 3A, 4, 8AC, 12AB, 13AB.

Secret numbers

Here are a few activities which can help children with reading, writing and ordering numbers to 100.

The 100 square

The object is to fill in the numbers on a '100 square'. The children can play this in a group.

What you need
Cards numbered from one to 100, pencils, a 10×10 grid of squares for each child.

What to do
Each child has his or her own 100 square to fill in, but the activity is done as a class. In turn, each child selects a card from the pack, and then reads out the number and shows it to the rest of the group. Then they can fill in the appropriate spaces on their

squares.

The children need not complete the 100 square in one session; in fact it would be an idea to stop them on occasions to discuss what they notice about the square. You might discuss the horizontal patterns, such as 43, 44, 45, 46, and the vertical patterns, 53, 63, 73, 83 – which leads on to adding and subtracting in tens. If the children come across an empty square they can be asked to predict what would fit in there.

Wiggly lines

This is a game for two players.

What you need
A 'wiggly line' board (as illustrated), coloured pencils of two different colours, one for each player, ten cards, each bearing a number between one and 100.

What to do
The cards are shuffled and placed face down on the table. Player 1 takes the top card, reads the number and decides on a position on the lines on which to place the number. Player 2 then has his turn. Play continues in this way, and in the end the player who has positioned all his numbers in the correct order is the winner.

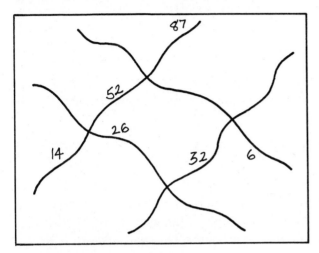

Find the number

This activity can be played with a group of children or against a computer; the relevant computer program is called *Find Me* (MEP Primary Maths Pack).

What you need
A number line to 100.

What do do
If the game is played with a group of children rather than against a computer, one child determines the number. She then writes the number on a card and puts the card in a safe place. The other children take it in turns to guess the number, and are given clues such as 'too small' or 'too big'. The children will probably need a number line up to 100 in front of them to refer to at some stage.

The computer program has a more difficult version as well, in which the following clues are given:
- Less than 5 away – hot.
- Less than 10 away – warm.
- Less than 20 away – cold.
- 20 or more away – freezing.

These clues could also be used without a computer.

Dot-to-dot pictures

Dot-to-dot pictures are invaluable for experience with counting and ordering numbers.

Essential language
Numbers to 100, count, order, more than, greater than, less than, smaller than.

ATs 2A.

Tuneful numbers

Various number line activities can be used to develop many different aspects of number work; for example, ordering numbers, sequential patterns, counting on, counting back and number bonds. Here is one variation based on the party game 'Musical chairs'.

What you need
A number line large enough for the children to walk on, made from a strip of durable material, and divided into ten squares. Each square should be marked with a number from one to ten using a permanent marker.

What to do
Ask ten children to pick a number on the line and stand on it. The children progress up the number line and back round to the start; any remaining children who cannot fit on the line can help form a circuit back to the start, so that everyone gets a turn as the game progresses.

Music is played as in 'Musical chairs'. When the music stops some of the children will be standing on a number. At this point, children are called out by the teacher or by another child according to various categories; for example, those standing on an odd or an even number, a number greater than or less than five, or a multiple of a certain number.

Essential language
Odd, even, less than, more than, add to, take away from.

ATs 2A, 3A.

Boxes

This game is available as computer programs under the titles *Boxes 1, 2, 3* and *4*. The supplier is ESM, Abbeygate House, East Road, Cambridge. The same game can also be played away from the computer as shown here. The game can help children to read, write and order numbers, to use the knowledge that the tens digit indicates the number of tens, and to compare greater and smaller numbers.

What you need
A set of ten cards numbered zero to nine, a board for each child as shown.

Tens	Units

What to do
Playing in pairs, the children shuffle the cards carefully and place them face down on the table. They then take turns to select one card at a time and place it on the board. The aim is to make the largest possible number, and once a card is placed it cannot be removed.

Here is an example of a game in which the second child is the winner.

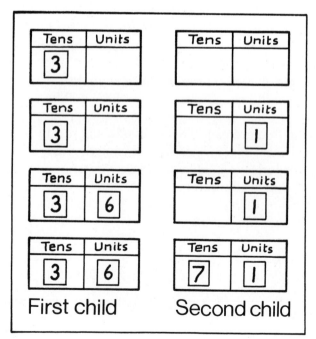

First child   Second child

Variations
There are a number of ways of extending this game.
- Try to make the smallest possible number.
- Include hundreds in the game as well as tens and units.
- Use more boards for each player.
- Include addition in the game, arranging the boards in this way.
- Change the way the game is played and the way the boards are set out. Prior knowledge of the symbols < and > is needed here.

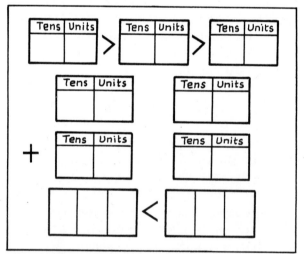

In this version of the game, Player A begins. A numbered card is selected and placed in one of the boxes. Player A has four turns filling all the spaces before the other player begins. In order to score two points the resulting number sentence must be true. Player B goes next, and after several rounds the total score is worked out.

- A further variation, instead of using the boards, is to place two chairs (one representing tens, the other representing units) for children to sit on. Cards can be selected in the same way, and held up by the children.

Essential language
Tens, units, greater than, less than, larger, largest, smaller, smallest.

ATs 2A.

48

Bingo

Achieving a quick recall of number bonds requires plenty of practice. To help create a positive attitude to mathematics, let the children practise with a variety of fun activities and games.

Bingo is aimed at developing the children's ability to add and subtract numbers to ten, and to compare two numbers and find the difference.

What you need

A Bingo card each, a pack of cards with simple number sentences without answers, eight counters each.

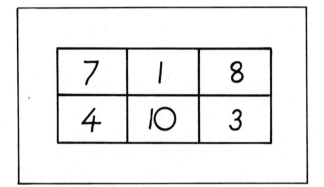

What to do

Elect one child as caller. The caller then shuffles the pack of number sentence cards and places them face down on the table. He or she selects the top card and reads it, placing it face up on the table. A player who has the correct answer on her Bingo card can place a counter on the appropriate square. The first player to fill her card with counters is the winner.

Variation

A variation on this would be to put the number sentences on the players' own Bingo cards. This would mean that every card turned over from the pack would contain just one number from one to ten, and any player whose card contained a number sentence whose answer came up could fill the appropriate square.

Essential language

Add, take away, subtract, more than, less than, count on, count back.

ATs 3AB.

e.g. for 7 → 3 + 4

8 less 1   6 more than 1

Straws

The idea that one ten is equivalent to ten units needs to be built up gradually. So too does the idea that the three in 37 represents three tens or 30 units. Situations where the children have to regroup numbers into tens and units are a useful aid.

What you need

Straws, elastic bands, a pack of cards numbered one to nine, an abacus, and a counting board.

What to do

This is a game for two players, and each child has five turns. The cards are shuffled and placed face down on the table. A player takes a card and collects the appropriate number of straws, which are then placed in the units column on the board.

When ten straws have been collected, they are bundled together with an elastic band and placed in the tens column on the counting board. After five turns each, the winners count their final score.

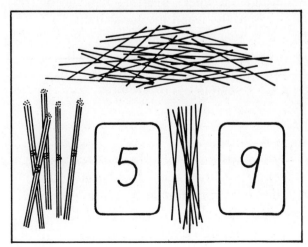

Whoever has the largest score is the winner; or alternatively the winner could be the person who is nearest to a certain number, such as 25.

The next stage would be to play the game using a spiked abacus together with a counting board. The children record the results both on the abacus and numerically, which reinforces the idea that the size of a digit is indicated by its position.

Variation

Play a similar game using subtraction. Using the abacus, the children could begin with two tens, and then as numbers are selected they could be taken away from 20. The person with the lowest number after five turns is the winner.

Essential language

Units, ones, tens, exchange, add on, take away, abacus, counting board, total, score.

ATs 2A, 3A.

Combos

Combos is an investigation the children can try in order to explore the patterns in addition and subtraction.

What you need

Joinable building cubes, pencils, paper.

What to do

Ask the children to select five cubes. They can then fix the cubes together and build a shape from them. Ask them to count the cubes again to check that they have used all five, and then split the construction in two. How many cubes have they removed? How many cubes are there left? Can they record what they have done in the form of a number sentence? For example,

- $3+2=5$

or

- $5-3=2$

(For the purpose of the investigation it is less confusing for the children to use *either* addition *or* subtraction for recording each manoeuvre).

Let the children place the cubes back

together again, and then try another way of separating them. Can they find a different way? Ask them to record what they have found.

Let them carry on taking the cubes apart, recording what they have found and piecing them back together. How many different ways can they find of taking the cubes apart?

When the children have found as many different ways as they can of splitting the cubes, they can put the number sentences in the following order; it will help them to explore the patterns more fully and also include any they have missed out.

- $5+0=5$
- $4+1=5$
- $3+2=5$
- $2+3=5$
- $1+4=5$
- $0+5=5$

Variations

You can vary this activity by trying the following suggestions:

- Split the constructions three different ways.
- Vary the original total number of cubes.
- Use subtraction for recording instead of addition.

Essential language

Numbers, plus, minus.

ATs 5A.

Making boxes

The task here is to explore the different nets of a cube. This involves appreciation of the properties of a cube and its faces, and the recognition of different types of movement, notably rotation and reflection.

What you need

Empty boxes and packets, scissors, rulers, squared paper, commercial construction sets.

What to do

Start by taking a look at a range of cubes and cuboids that are used for packaging. The children will then be able to see the

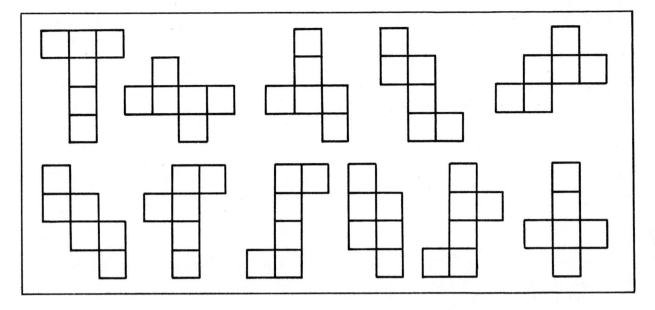

connection between the investigation and the task that manufacturers have in producing boxes and packets.

Take some empty cube-shaped boxes and cut them open down the sides so that you can see how many faces they have, and the shape of each face. Once the children have found out the number of faces a cube has, the investigation can begin.

Use a construction set containing interlocking shapes, such as Polydron or Clixi. Ask the children to select six squares and lock them together to make a cube. Then they can unfold it and open it out flat, making sure that the six squares are connected. The shape they have made is called a net.

Next, the children can copy the net on to 2cm squared paper, and then put the cube back together again and unfold it to make a different net. Ask the children to find out how many different nets they can make.

If rotations and reflections are eliminated, the solutions are as follows:

Variation
A similar task can be carried out with a cuboid, or a tetrahedron made of interlocking triangles.

Essential language
Cube, square, cuboid, oblong, tetrahedron, triangular pyramid, triangle, face, edge, shape, net.

ATs 10A, 11C.

Tree measurements

Trees provide plenty of scope for children to practise their skills of measurement. Record the results obtained on tables, charts and graphs.

What you need
Tape-measures, rulers, strips of paper, string.

What to do
Tell the children that they are going to measure the girth of a tree. Let them decide what they are going to use to do this; they may want to use strips of paper, string, cubits or handspans. Get them to estimate first, and ask them for suggestions for the design of a data collection sheet on which to record their results.

After measuring, to what extent do the children's results vary? Can they suggest any reasons for the variations? Do they have any suggestions to make to rectify this? They may be able to suggest the use of the appropriate standard measure.

Measure the girth of other trees. How far up the tree trunk are the children measuring the girth? Is it always in the same place on each tree? If not, should it be? Does it make a difference? These are questions for the children to think about. Ideally the girth of each tree should be measured about one metre up.

The children can also measure the lengths of the leaves and the spread of the branches. They can also suggest ways of measuring the area of the leaves by drawing round a leaf, then trying various objects to cover the leaf shape. Which object do they think fits best? Always make sure that the children have ample opportunity to estimate first before carrying out the actual measurements, and then a chance to compare their estimates with the results.

Essential language
Estimate, measure, length, area, distance, girth, longer than, shorter than, handspans, cubits, metres, centimetres.

ATs 1ABC, 8AC, 9ABC, 12B, 13A.

Windmill

The children will have to consider a wide range of mathematical questions in designing and making their own windmills.

What you need
A selection of junk materials including plastic and cardboard containers, sheets of card and paper, scissors, pens and pencils, paper-fasteners, sticky tape, adhesive.

What to do
Begin this activity by taking the children outside to have a look at the effects of a windy day on such things as trees, leaves, smoke, plants and washing on a line. Let them carry out their observations on a number of occasions and make comparisons.

Then ask the children to design and construct a windmill in order to measure wind speed. Working as a group or in pairs, ask them to discuss and consider what would be the best way of tackling this.

They can select what they need from a range of materials, and they should produce a design which can be made into a working model.

Encourage the children to consider the problem from many angles; for example, what size are they going to make the sails? What type of paper are they going to use?

They can then set about constructing the windmill using the appropriate mathematics. They will need to take some

measurements. How are they going to do this? What are they going to use? Once the windmill is made, they can test whether it works efficiently, modify it and, if necessary, remake it.

Next the children can use the models to measure the wind speed. Encourage them to collate and record their results. The results can be compared across the groups; this may lead to the children considering further refinement of their models. They can also investigate whether or not it makes any difference to the direction in which the sails spin if they hold the model so that it faces different directions.

Essential language
Eight point of the compass, seconds, minutes.

ATs 1ABC, 2A, 3B, 12B, 13A.

Fill it up

These activities address Attainment Target 8, and are concerned with volume and capacity. The children have a chance to compare the different containers by filling and emptying them, and the activity will help them recognise the need to use standard measures.

What you need
Various containers – cups, jugs, troughs, thimbles, teaspoons, jars, squeezy bottles; and fillers such as water, sand, sawdust and marbles.

What to do
Ask the children to estimate which container holds the most and which holds the least. Let them sort and order the containers according to their estimated capacity.

Compare the containers by filling and emptying them. Estimate and discover how many cups can be filled from a jug, and how many eggcups, teacups and beakers. This will help the children recognise the need to use a standard measure.

Introduce the litre as a fixed quantity of liquid which may be held in different

containers. Sort the containers into sets, estimating and discovering those which will hold more or less than a litre. Find the capacity of a bucket by using a litre jug. Introduce other measures by finding the bucket's capacity using a half-litre measure, a quarter-litre measure, a 100 ml measure, and so on.

Introduce volume by using transparent containers filled with different objects, such as marbles, beads, cubes and so on. The different fillers can be compared by looking at the size of the spaces they leave between them in the containers. This will eventually lead to recognising the need for a standard unit of measurement; a three-dimensional shape that fits together without gaps.

Essential language
Full, empty, high, low, half full, half empty, container, large, larger than, largest, small, smaller than, smallest, fill, estimate, holds more, holds less, holds most, holds least, capacity, sort, put in order, no spaces, large spaces, small spaces, tiny spaces, match, container, compare, how many, discovery, eggcupfuls, pictogram, measure, litre, half-litre, quarter-litre.

ATs 1ABC, 2A, 8AC.

Halving and quartering

An understanding of the meaning of halving and quartering is best achieved by cutting objects into the relevant sized pieces. Let the children cut up some fruit or cake, look at the pieces, discuss the number of halves and the number of quarters and place them back together to make a whole. This experience can be reinforced further through the following activities.

Picture cards

This activity reinforces the idea of reflective symmetry, and can be extended to include quarters as well as halves.

What you need
A set of cards with pictures which are symmetrical; a tree, a butterfly, a face, a house etc. The cards should be cut in half along the line of symmetry.

What to do
Ask pairs of children to shuffle the cards and place them in a pile on the table. They take it in turns to select a card from the top of the pack. When they have a whole picture they place the cards together face upwards on the table. The child with the greater number of whole pictures is the winner.

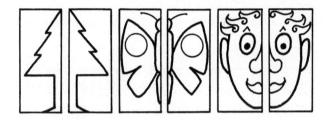

Halving squares

Try this activity, which is based on halving squares, and which can also be extended to quartering.

What you need
Squared paper with large squares; coloured pencils.

What to do
Ask the children to try to find as many ways of colouring in *half* a square as they can.

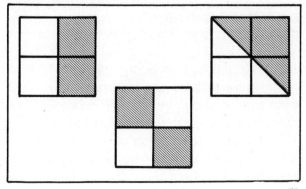

Once they have found as many different ways as possible of halving the squares ask the children to compare their results to see if any are similar. They may decide that if they rotate or reflect the shapes then some of the ways they have found of colouring them in are similar. They may decide to eliminate the similar squares, or to keep them. Whichever is the case, looking for rotations and reflections is a worthwhile addition to this investigation.

There are many different solutions to this problem.

Variations

Try the same activity with quartering squares, or with halving or quartering oblongs. Experiment with halving different shapes by using isometric paper for the activity instead of squared paper.

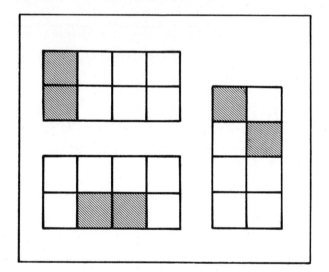

Essential language

Half, halved, quarter, square, oblong, shape, triangle, turn, rotate, flip over, reflect.

ATs 1ABC, 2B, 9ABC, 10A, 11C.

Coloured kites

This investigation is concerned with discovering the number of possible arrangements of colours on a quartered kite.

What you need

Squared paper, isometric paper, coloured pencils or crayons.

54

What to do

Ask the children to draw a kite with four squares.

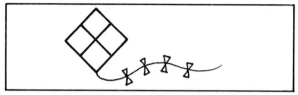

Let them use yellow and red crayons to colour the squares, using only one colour per square. Then ask them to draw some more kites and colour them in a different arrangement, again using the yellow and red crayons. How many different ways can they colour the kites?

Encourage the children to rotate (turn) and reflect (flip over) the kites they have already coloured in to find other arrangements. It may be necessary to point out to the children that a kite may be all one colour. Counting kites of all one colour and rotations and reflections, there are 16 different arrangements altogether.

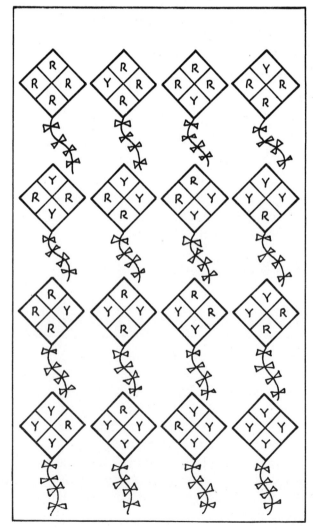

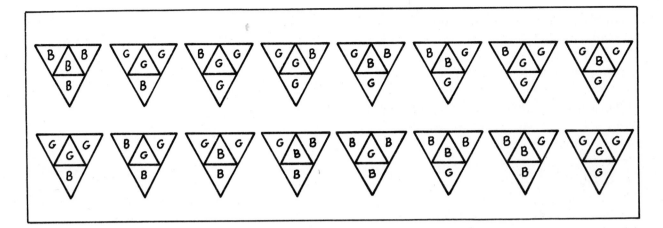

Variation

Draw kites with triangles, this time using isometric paper. Use two colours as before, and find different ways of colouring the triangular kites. How many different ways can the children find? (In fact there are also 16 different ways to colour these kites.)

You might also consider letting the children make 'real' kites, following perhaps some of the four-way designs already tried. Making a full-scale kite would involve measuring skills, and when finished the kites could be tested and their efficacy compared.

Essential language

Square, triangle, differences, rotate, turn, reflect, flip over.

ATs 2B, 9ABC, 11C.

Leaf shapes

These activities involve the following skills: understanding the notion of angle; giving and understanding instructions for turning through right angles; recognising the differences between translation, rotation and reflection.

What you need

A variety of leaves, card, scissors, paper, pens, paints, paper-fasteners; for the variation, clay, slip, a blunt knife.

What to do

Begin by looking at some different leaves. Discuss their shape; are the leaves single or compound, do they have jagged, smooth or rounded edges?

Let the children each select one leaf to work with, and draw round it on card to make a template of the leaf shape.

Provide each of the children with a square piece of paper whose sides are at least twice as long as the length of their leaf.

Fold the square in half, and then into quarters, and open it out.

After checking that the leaf template fits into each quarter of the square, the children can try making the following patterns.
● Draw around the leaf shape, then slide it across into the next square to create a translated leaf pattern.
● Draw round the leaf template, then turn it through a right angle to rotate the leaf shape pattern. (Fix one end of the leaf shape to the centre of the square using a paper-fastener.)
● Make a pattern by rotating the leaf shape through 360 degrees, drawing round it at regular intervals.

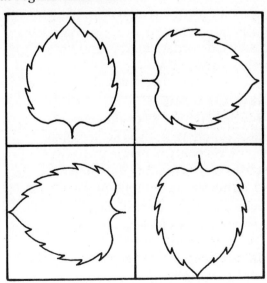

- Fold a rectangular piece of paper in half. Place the leaf shape on one side and draw round it. Then flip the leaf shape over to create a reflected pattern and draw round it again.

These patterns can be created in a variety of media, such as paint, printing and wax crayons.

Variation

Make clay tiles by rolling out pieces of clay to about one centimetre in thickness. Use either a square tile cutter or a blunt knife to cut squares from the clay. Roll out some thinner pieces of clay and use them to make leaf shapes. Fix the leaf shapes on to the squares using slip. When complete, make holes in the tiles so that they can be hung up to create a display. If the holes are made in different sides of the tiles the display can also show rotation.

Essential language

Half, quarter, angle, right angle, turn, rotate, flip over, reflect, slide across, translate.

ATs 11ABC.

Make a monster

Ask the children to make a three-dimensional monster; perhaps a model of a monster from one of their own stories or games.

This activity is designed to accommodate the following statements of attainment: recognise and describe two- and three-dimensional shapes; recognise right-angled corners in two- and three-dimensional shapes.

What you need

A wide selection of three-dimensional shapes; cylinders such as sweet tubes, toilet- or kitchen-roll centres, straws; cuboids such as stock cube containers, tea and toothpaste packets; triangular prisms such as Toblerone boxes; and some cones and spheres if available.

What to do

Discuss the properties of the shapes. Begin

by asking the children to sort the shapes into cylinders, cuboids etc. Then ask them to take each collection separately and sort, compare, classify and order the objects in as many different ways as possible, noting similarities and differences.

Play a game by asking the children to pick up a shape which has a specific property, for example a curved surface, or the ability to slide along.

When the three-dimensional shapes are grouped in families of solids, the children can cover and decorate the surfaces, and use the shapes to design a model of a monster. The models could be free-standing or strung together to make a mobile.

Encourage the children to use just one basic shape to make each monster, so that one is made from cylinders, another from cuboids, another from triangular prisms, and so on.

Variation

This activity also works with two-dimensional shapes. Provide the children with a collection of two-dimensional shapes of different sizes; squares, rectangles, circles, triangles, pentagons, hexagons and so on. Ask them to sort, compare, classify and order the shapes. Discuss the criteria used and note similarities and differences. Then the activity can proceed as with three-dimensional shapes.

When the children are sorting the two- and three-dimensional shapes, they can also practise recognising right angles. Children can check that a shape has a right angle by using a guide made from paper. They will need to fold a square of paper in half once, and then again, so that the folded edges lie together, taking care to obtain a good right angle.

Children's ability to recognise right angles will also be reinforced through PE activities which involve them in turning through right angles. Stress that they should be able to recognise right angles in different orientations.

Essential language
Shape, solid, plane, faces, vertex, vertices, edges, corners, slide, roll, right angle, curved, straight, surface, square, rectangle, circle, triangle, hexagon, pentagon, cube, cuboid, cylinder, sphere.

ATs 10AB.

Blind man's buff

Blind man's buff can give the children an opportunity to practise their understanding of angles. They will also have a chance to give and act upon instructions for turning through right angles. This activity works best in a large space such as a hall or gymnasium. It could be incorporated into a PE lesson.

What you need
Blindfolds; pieces of paper to make an 'obstacle course'.

What to do
The children need to be in pairs, one giving and the other receiving and carrying out instructions. The latter could be blindfold if desired.

The child giving instructions can plot out a course for the other child, who has to turn through right angles and walk forwards or backwards to get from one location to another.

An 'obstacle course' could be arranged; for safety try just placing pieces of paper on the floor to mark out certain areas. Instructions can be given in order to manoeuvre a partner round the course.

Allow the children to develop their own system for recording the instructions, and let them draw a plan of the course.

Variation
A similar activity can be carried out using a floor turtle. Using a concept keyboard in conjunction with the floor turtle, you can create overlays to make the programming of instructions easier. An obstacle course can also be designed for the turtle.

Essential language
Right angle, 90°, 180°, left, right.

ATs 11AB.

What's the chance?

Use discussion times and normal day-to-day classroom situations to develop children's ability to understand, estimate and calculate probabilities.

For example, is it certain:
- that it will rain tomorrow?
- that we will eat our dinner at 12 o'clock midday?
- that we will have our breakfast at midnight?

This can form the basis of a game.

What you need
A board showing three coloured boxes, one saying 'Impossible', one saying 'Don't know', and the other saying 'Certain', and a pack of blank cards.

What to do
On each of the cards, write a question the answer to which is either 'Impossible', 'Don't know', or 'Certain'. Put a dot of the colour corresponding to the appropriate box on the board on the back of each card.

Some possible questions which could go on the cards are:
- Will the sun shine tomorrow?
- Will I be two tomorrow?
- Will I eat my dinner today?
- Will I go to bed tonight?
- Will I play with my friends at playtime?
- Will it get dark tonight?
- Will it rain tomorrow?
- Will I be 50 tomorrow?
- If I shake a die will I throw a two?

Arrange the cards in a pile with the statement uppermost. The children can play the game in small groups taking it in turns to take a card from the top of the pack, reading the statement then placing the card in the appropriate box. The cards can be checked afterwards using the coloured dot on the back.

Essential language
Chance, impossible, don't know, uncertain, certain, definitely will not happen, will happen, may or may not happen.

ATs 14.

Trains

'Trains' can be played with or without a computer. It involves addition, subtraction, and reading numbers to 100. It also demands a method of trial and improvement, and requires planning ahead. (The *Trains* program is on a disc called 'Number Games', available from ESM, Abbeygate House, East Road, Cambridge.)

What you need
Pictures of a train with empty carriages, joinable cubes to help with counting, pens and pencils.

What to do
In this game the children are asked to fill the carriages on a train with people. They must put some people in each carriage, using only the numbers they are given.

For example, they could be required to solve this problem:
'Fill the train with 14 people.
You can use fives or twos, and there are four carriages to be filled.'

Players may attempt an easy, average or hard version of the game. An example of the average version on the computer program is as follows:
'Fill the train with 40 people.

You can use fours or sixes, and there are eight carriages.'

When the children have worked out the answer, they can draw that number of passengers in the empty carriages.

Variation
This problem can be turned into an investigation where there are many possible answers. Ask the children to make a given number using numbers of their own choice. The only limitation is how many numbers they can use.

Encourage the children to look for different solutions to the same problem in order to explore the possibilities of different combinations of numbers and number patterns. Allowing children to use a calculator to do this helps them to focus their attention on the problem.

Essential language
Add, count on, take away, greater than, less than.

ATs 2A, 3AB.

Squirrel run

The purpose of this game is to develop the ability to distinguish between odd and even numbers. The players aim to be the first to run to the top of the tree and reach the food store.

What you need
Two counters of different colours, a 'Squirrel run' board (see photocopiable page 178), a die, joinable cubes.

What to do
Each player throws a die in turn. The players move up the tree one step at a time, by throwing an even number. If an odd number is thrown there is no move. The children may use cubes here to check whether a number is odd or even. If the

number is even they will be able to make two towers of equal height.

The first player to reach the food store is the winner.

Alternatively, after reaching the top you can carry on with the game and move back down, but the rules are different; a player can only move down if an odd number is thrown.

Variation

More than one die can be used. The players throw the dice and add or subtract the score. They then have to decide whether the answer is odd or even before they can move.

Essential language

Odd, even, add, sum, total, equal to, difference, take away.

ATs 3AB, 5B.

Hop it

'Hop it' is a calculator game for two players. It gives practice in finding the difference between numbers from one to twenty by adding on or counting back, and making use of a symbol to stand for an unknown number.

The object of the activity is to be the first to reach the lily-pad by taking turns to hop from stone to stone.

What you need

Coloured counters, cards numbered one to twenty, and a 'Hop it' board (see photocopiable page 179).

What to do

Shuffle the pack of cards and place it face down. Each player places his or her counter on a frog.

At each 'go' a player turns over the top card, which might for example be a 12. To move to the next numbered rock the player has to find the difference between the number on the card and the number on the rock, which might be six. The player predicts the answer and then checks using the calculator.

- Thinks: $12-6=6$
- Checks: $12-6=6$

If the estimate is correct, the player moves to the next rock. If incorrect, they cannot move forward.

The winner is the first to hop across all the rocks and reach the finish.

Essential language

Equal to, sum, difference, add, result, subtract.

ATs 3AB, 6.

Shopping activities

The following activities give practice with various aspects of money, particularly the idea of getting change.

Spending money

This game gives the children practice in exchanging ten 10p pieces for £1.

What you need

A die marked in tens, a box of 10p tokens, a box of £1 tokens, jigsaws as illustrated for each child.

What to do

Elect one child to be the banker. The die is thrown by a player, who takes the appropriate number of ten pence pieces or tokens. When they have collected enough they can exchange their ten 10p pieces for a £1 coin. They can then buy any one of the five items using this money. Each item must be paid for using a £1 coin. The first player to collect all five items is the winner.

Chance shopping

'Chance shopping' is a money game using addition and subtraction with amounts less than £1.

What you need

10p pieces, set of 20 chance cards similar to those illustrated.

dolls house **80p**

pencils cost **5p** each

tennis racket **20p**

car **10p**

balls one ball costs **30p**

Chance Shopping

umbrella **5p**

engine **40p**

doll **50p**

yacht **60p**

snake **20p**

What to do
Place the chance cards face down in a pile on the table.

Each player in turn takes a card, and when they have given the correct answer they take a 10p coin from the box. Used cards are placed in a discard pile, and the child with the most money at the end of the game is the winner.

Essential language
Spend, cost, pay, buy, coin, pence, the same as, more than, less than, change, total, charge, twice as much, half, half as much.

ATs 2A, 3ABC, 8B.

Buy a juggler

This game requires the children to use their skills of coin recognition, combining amounts and giving change.

What you need
For each player, the parts of a juggler and a juggler board (see photocopiable page 180), plastic money, die marked 1p, 1p, 1p, 2p, 2p, 5p.

What to do
The aim of the game is to buy a juggler, a piece at a time. Each piece has a specific value.

First, elect a child to be banker. The players take turns to throw the die, and win the amount shown on the uppermost face.

The children collect their winnings in coins, and can then start to buy their jugglers. Savings will have to be made before some purchases can be made.

The first player to buy the complete juggler is the winner.

Variations
● Change the cost of each part of the juggler to larger amounts. You will also need to raise the amounts on the die, or use two dice, in which case the children will have to combine the amounts on the dice correctly before collecting their winnings.

● Another variation would be to use two dice, and to ask the children to find the difference between the amounts on the dice. When the correct answer is given the children collect their winnings as before.

● Develop the children's skills of coin recognition by sticking the relevant coins themselves to the various parts of the juggler, and use a correspondingly marked die.

Essential language
Pence, coin, add, subtract, take away, find the difference, change.

ATs 2A, 3ABC, 8B.

Level 2 glossary of terms

The following glossary explains some of the mathematical terms which are contained within the statements of attainment for mathematics at Level 2.

Carroll diagram
A matrix or array for the classification of objects according to two criteria or attributes. Named after Lewis Carroll.

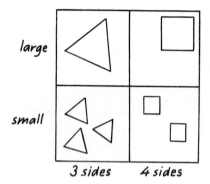

Data collection sheet
A sheet usually ruled into columns for the collection of numerical information; for example, a tally chart for a traffic survey.

Vehicles	Tally	Total
cars	JHT JHT I	11
buses	III	3
lorries	JHT I	6
vans	JHT III	8
coaches	II	2

Digit
A figure or symbol which represents a number, or forms part of a number.

Frequency table
A table that summarises the frequencies for a set of observations.

Vehicles	Mon	Tue	Wed	Thur	Fri	Total
cars	11					
buses	3					
lorries	6					
vans	8					
coaches	2					

Mathematics
The study of patterns and relationships between objects and the means of communicating these. Mathematics involves the proving or deriving of such patterns and relationships through the use of logic.

Oblongs and rectangles
An oblong is a rectangle having adjacent sides that are unequal. A rectangle is a four-sided shape with four right angles. Thus, the set of rectangles includes both oblongs and squares.

To avoid confusing the children, use the term oblong rather than rectangle when describing a four-sided shape with four right angles and adjacent sides unequal.

Non-standard measures
Also referred to as arbitrary units. These are units not generally accepted as measures, which are nevertheless used for measuring quantities. They may be of a standard size, such as straws (for measuring length), bottle tops (for weighing) or yoghurt pots (for finding capacities), or they may vary from one person to the other, as in the case of body measures such as cubits and handspans.

Reflection
A mirror-image of a shape produced by 'flipping over'.

Rotation
An image of a shape produced by 'turning'.

Symbol
A letter, numeral or sign which is used to represent a number, an operation or any other mathematical idea.

Translation
An image of a shape produced by 'sliding'.

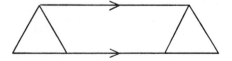

Level 2: Programme of Study

This diagram shows how the programme of study can be expanded, suggesting teaching stages where applicable.

- Commutative aspect of addition: 7+3=10; 3+7=10.
- Number bonds to 20.
- Add with money up to 20p.
- Record addition and subtraction by different methods.
- Work out simple shopping bills.
- Find the difference by matching and counting on.
- Give change.
- Explore the relationship between adding on and taking away.
- Subtract by counting back.
- Apply the idea of counting back to taking away.
- Subtract with money.

- Enter the total number of members of a set into boxes.
- Fill a box at the end of a number statement.
- Select the correct member of a universal set to enter into an open sentence.
- Understand the inverse relationship of addition and subtraction.

- Recognise coins in use.
- Make up coin amounts to 10p, 20p and £1.

- Match two-dimensional shapes with the same shape and size.
- Sort two- and three-dimensional shapes into sets by name.
- Assess the properties of two- and three-dimensional shapes – number of edges and corners etc.
- Match two-dimensional shapes to the faces of the relevant three-dimensional shapes.

- Explore the differences in shapes when they are rotated, translated or reflected.
- Make patterns by translating, rotating or reflecting a shape.

Using and applying mathematics
- Select the materials and the mathematics to use for a practical task.
- Describe work and check results.
- Ask and respond to the question: 'What would happen if . . .?'

Number
- Read, write and order numbers to at least 100, and use the knowledge that the tens digit indicates the number of tens.
- Understand the meaning of 'half' and 'quarter'.
- Know and use addition and subtraction facts up to ten.
- Compare two numbers to find the difference.
- Solve whole number problems involving addition and subtraction, including money.
- Make a sensible estimate of a number of objects up to 20.

Algebra
- Explore and use patterns in addition and subtraction facts to ten.
- Distinguish odd and even numbers.
- Understand the use of a symbol to stand for an unknown number.

Measures
- Use non-standard measures in length, area, volume, capacity, 'weight' and time, comparing objects and recognising the need for standard units.
- Use coins in simple contexts.
- Know commonly used units in length, capacity, 'weight' and time.

Shape and space
- Recognise squares, rectangles, circles, triangles, hexagons, pentagons, cubes, rectangular boxes (cuboids), cylinders and spheres, and describe them.
- Understand the notion of angle.
- Understand turning through right angles and recognise right-angled corners.
- Recognise types of movement: straight (translation), turning (rotation) and flip (reflection).

Handling data
- Choose criteria to sort and classify objects; record results or outcomes of events.
- Design a data collection sheet recording data leading to a frequency table.
- Construct and interpret frequency tables and block graphs.
- Use diagrams to represent the result of classification using two different criteria.
- Recognise a degree of uncertainty about the outcomes of some events and that other events are certain or impossible.

- Count on in twos, threes and fours to 20.
- Early grouping games and activities.
- Group in tens.
- Number line activities.

- Divide objects into halves and quarters.
- Partition sets.
- Tell the time in half and quarter hours.

- Find the difference between numbers by counting on with objects such as cubes, or counting back along number lines.

- Number bonds.
- Understand the commutative and associative aspects of addition.
- Understand the inverse relationship of addition and subtraction.

- Use arbitrary measures.
- Measure to the nearest arbitrary units.
- Use a smaller arbitrary measure to record what is left over when using larger units.
- Develop an idea of the need for a standard unit of measure.

- Understand standard metric measures.
- Compare objects against standard metric measures.
- Compare objects against standard Imperial measures.
- Compare objects against halves of standard measures.

- Turn through one, two, three and four right angles to face north, east, west and south.
- Make and use a paper right angle to identify other right angles.

Level 2 : attainment targets 1–6

Use this chart to check which attainment targets are covered by each activity.

ACTIVITY	1			2		3			4	5		6
	A	B	C	A	B	A	B	C		A	B	
School meals	▲	▲	▲			•	•					
Break-times	▲	▲	▲	•								
At the shop				•		•	•	•				
Looking after living things	•	•	•	•		•						
Time				•		•	•					
Past times	•	•	•	▲								
Seeds and fruit	•	•	•	•	•	•			▲			
Secret numbers				▲								
Tuneful numbers				▲		•						
Boxes				▲								
Bingo						▲	•					
Straws				▲		•						
Combos										▲		
Making boxes												
Tree measurements	•	•	•									
Windmill	▲	▲	▲	•			•					
Fill it up	•	•	•	•								
Halving and quartering	•	•	•		▲							
Coloured kites					•							
Leaf shapes												
Make a monster												
Blind man's buff												
What's the chance?												
Trains				•		▲	▲					
Squirrel run						•	•			▲		
Hop it						•	•					▲
Shopping activities				•		•	•	▲				
Buy a juggler				•		•	•	•				

Key: • = touches on
     ▲ = especially relevant

Level 2 : attainment targets 8–14

Use this chart to check which attainment targets are covered by each activity.
(There is no Attainment Target 7 at Level 2.)

ACTIVITY	8 A	8 B	8 C	9 A	9 B	9 C	10 A	10 B	11 A	11 B	11 C	12 A	12 B	13 A	13 B	14
School meals												•	•	•	•	
Break-times	•		•	•		•										
At the shop		▲														
Looking after living things	•		•	▲	▲	▲						•	•	•		
Time	▲		▲													
Past times				•	•							•	•	•	•	
Seeds and fruit	▲		▲									•	•	•	•	
Secret numbers																
Tuneful numbers																
Boxes																
Bingo																
Straws																
Combos																
Making boxes							•				▲					
Tree measurements	▲		▲	•	•	•						•	•			
Windmill												•	•			
Fill it up																
Halving and quartering				•	•	•	•				•					
Coloured kites				•	•	•					▲					
Leaf shapes									▲	▲	▲					
Make a monster							▲	▲								
Blind man's buff									▲	▲						
What's the chance?																▲
Trains																
Squirrel run																
Hop it																
Shopping activities		▲														
Buy a juggler		▲														

Key: • = touches on
      ▲ = especially relevant

Level 2 : Contexts

This chart shows the wider contexts of each activity.

ACTIVITY	Everyday situations	Everyday problems	Games and fun	Maths problems	Maths investigations	Calculator activities	Computer activities	English (Core)	Science (Core)	Art (Foundation)	PE	History	Geography	Music	Technology	Local Curriculum	RE	Possible topic link	School-wide themes
School meals	•								•										•
Break-times		•																	
At the shop	•		•	•															
Looking after living things		•							•							•		•	
Time					•							•						•	
Past times							•					•	•			•		•	
Seeds and fruit									•				•			•		•	•
Secret numbers			•	•			•												
Tuneful numbers			•											•					
Boxes			•				•												
Bingo			•	•															
Straws			•																
Combos					•														
Making boxes					•														
Tree measurements					•				•									•	
Windmill									•	•	•				•			•	
Fill it up					•														
Halving and quartering					•														
Coloured kites					•														
Leaf shapes					•					•	•							•	
Make a monster			•							•					•				
Blind man's buff			•								•								
What's the chance?			•		•														
Trains			•	•			•												•
Squirrel run			•	•															
Hop it			•	•		•													
Shopping activities			•	•														•	
Buy a juggler			•																

Chapter three
Level 3

Introduction

This chapter contains a wide variety of suggestions for involving children in mathematical work within relevant and interesting contexts. The children will often get real benefit from topics which are of particular relevance to them, and which actually have an effect on their lives. This need not be an enormous undertaking; a number of mathematical techniques can be applied to simple projects, whether they involve the children in drawing up league tables for their own team games, or planning an end of term party. Children can get useful practice in amassing and using data by conducting surveys within the school, and there is a good deal of satisfaction to be gained from assessing the information generated.

Children at this level will benefit from exploring number patterns; investigations of this sort will help them see the beauty and fascination of numbers. There are also important things to be learned from practical activities such as cooking or inventing ways to measure rainfall or wind speed. Among the other activities for Level 3 are some intriguing games, many of which can involve the use of computers and calculators.

Journey to school

Wherever the school is, and however the children get there, the journey to school can provide a broad range of mathematical activity. Studying such journeys also provides an excellent way of introducing safety issues.

- Use a variety of street maps covering the catchment area of the school. The children could look at A-Z maps, teacher-prepared maps, and Ordnance Survey maps of different scales. Ask them to work out the direction of the school from their homes.
- Plot the homes of all the children in the group on a map. This could be extended to children in other groups within the school. The collection of the necessary information could involve surveys or the use of lists and registers.

- Use the resulting plan to investigate distribution patterns. Are most of the children's homes clustered near to the school? Is there a uniform spread in terms of distance to school? What is the position of the school in relation to its catchment area? Does it lie at the hub or nearer to the edge? In which direction do most children have to travel?
- Children at this level will probably have difficulty in understanding and visualising distances as great as a kilometre. However, if you draw circles radiating out from school to indicate distances of, say, half a kilometre and a whole kilometre, children could work out approximately whether their journeys were more or less than those distances.
- As journeys to school rarely follow a straight line, children could be asked to find out who lives closest to one kilometre

or half a kilometre from school. Walk the route with the children to give them concrete experience of this distance.

• Journeys may involve the chance of encountering various road hazards, such as getting out of the car, crossing roads, or turning across the flow of traffic. A survey of traffic density and flow could identify likely trouble spots. This could lead to suggestions for alternative routes.

When collecting data for a traffic survey the children will be encountering numbers up to 1000. They will also construct and interpret bar charts and pictograms and enter and access data in a simple computer database.

Essential language
Estimate, approximate, kilometre, metre, the eight points of the compass, data, interpret, symbol, bar chart, value, axis.

ATs 1ABC, 2A, 8ABC, 11B, 12AB, 13AB.

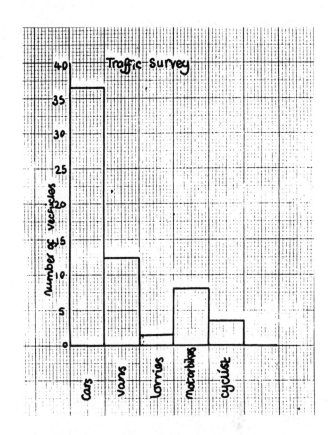

League tables

As part of a games programme the children could be encouraged to record results and draw up league tables. Games with limited players (like five-a-side) are a feature of many PE sessions, and give children the opportunity to practise a range of skills in different situations.

Games such as football, Unihoc, netball and volleyball are well known, but lesser-known activities such as three court end ball, permit ball and skittle ball are simple games of short duration which, as well as giving balance to a games programme, are suited to this particular activity. Children may also invent their own games or adapt popular games.

Football league tables have columns to show goals for and against, and similar tables can be made for other games. The recording of goals or points for and against their own teams will help children to appreciate negative and positive numbers. This Unihoc league table was drawn up by a nine-year-old.

Essential language
Negative, add, subtract, minus, deduct, take away.

ATs 2C, 3A.

Class 5's Unihoc League Table

	P	W	D	L	F	A	Pts	Goal Difference
Fulcons	6	4	2	0	20	10	10	+ 10
Hawks	6	2	3	1	16	14	7	+ 2
Kestrels	6	1	2	3	14	18	4	− 4
Eagles	6	0	3	3	12	20	3	− 8

Party time

There are many opportunities for parties to take place within the school year. They may celebrate a school event, or commemorate religious or cultural events such as Christmas, Diwali, Eid, Hanukkah, New Year, Baisakhi and so on.

Ask children to become involved in the planning and organisation of parties, and use it as a context for the use and application of mathematics.

When planning a party the children will need to survey the likes and dislikes of the party-goers in terms of food, drink, games and music. They can use the results of their surveys at the planning stage, and also as a justification for any decisions they have made.

The information they have gathered will help the children identify what food needs to be ordered.
- What can be made?
- What has to be bought?
- How much needs to be bought?
- How much will it cost?
- How much will each child have to contribute?

If the children make things to eat, they will be using appropriate units and instruments and interpreting the values of the numbers on measuring equipment.

Where items need to be bought, the children involved in the ordering will be required to multiply and divide, to understand remainders and whether to round up or down, and know how to work within the constraints of a budget.

Essential language
Estimate, multiply, divide, remainder, round up, round down, kilogramme, gramme, litre.

ATs 1ABC, 2B, 3BC, 4B, 8ABC, 9ABC, 12A, 13AB.

Food prices

From Level 2 onward children are required to perform calculations with money. They are set a number of tasks involving the addition, subtraction, multiplication and division of money. As a way of ensuring that the example prices used are realistic, create a database listing the prices of a number of things. This could be useful in a variety of ways.
- Teachers could refer to it as a way of ensuring that the prices they use in activities are realistic.
- It could be used by children when they are planning menus, making shopping lists

and budgeting.

• It provides children with a context for accessing information in a simple database.

• Children can have responsibility for entering and collecting information.

• In order to ensure that the information remains realistic it will need to be reviewed and updated by the children.

Some of these activities are appropriate to children at other levels, but the establishment of a simple but useful database could be handled by children at this level, perhaps using a database such as *Factfile*, available from the Cambridge University Press, which is a popular program because of its relative simplicity.

Essential language

Pounds, pence.

ATs 2B, 12AB.

Daily routines

Daily routines present numerous opportunities to use and apply mathematics and handle and present data, while at the same time supporting a health or personal and social education programme.

The following survey suggestions are by no means exhaustive, but they offer a number of starting points.

Mealtimes

• Do children eat meals at approximately the same times each day?

• Do they eat breakfast, and if so, what do they have?

• Do they eat supper, and if so what?

Snacks

• What sort of snacks do children eat?

• How often do they eat them?

• Do they have snacks at regular intervals throughout the day?

Bedtimes

• Do children always go to bed at approximately the same time?

• Does bedtime tend to be later on certain days?

• Which are the most common bedtimes among different age-groups?

Television

• Do children watch television for approximately the same length of time each day?

• How late do they watch?

• Do they have televisions in their own rooms?

• What are their favourite types of programme?

Pastimes

• What are the children's favourite pastimes?

• Are they carried out at home?

• Where do they play when they are outside?

• Are they members of clubs?

• How much time is spent in physical recreation?

Essential language

Bar chart, symbol, axis, value.

ATs 9ABC, 12AB, 13AB.

Weather records

Level 3 is an important transitional stage between pictorial representation and the use of more abstract symbols. Before reading a thermometer scale the children will adopt subjective estimates concerning heat; they will judge whether things are hot, warm, cool or cold. They might also be able to construct a range of arbitrary measures for wind speed and rainfall. Ways of measuring wind direction will pose technical problems whose solution will exercise mathematical skills of design and construction.

It is probable that at this stage children will be inventing their own symbols to record weather conditions, and records can be used to construct bar charts and pictograms.

The recording of weather data provides an opportunity to develop and use a relatively simple computer database in order to store, sort and compare information.

Due to the inconsistencies in the science and mathematics attainment targets with regard to the measurement of temperature (see page 6) it will be necessary for children to gather such information from secondary sources such as radio, television and newspapers. They could also use computer programs like *Science Start Here! – Weather* (ITV), which also contains past records which can be accessed to provide data for comparison. Alternatively, the children could be encouraged to construct their own database in order to record their first-hand observations.

Essential language
Centimetre, eight points of the compass.

ATs 1ABC, 8AB, 9ABC, 11B, 12AB, 13AB.

Investigating soils

At Level 3 of Science Attainment Target 9 children are required to give an account of an investigation into rocks or soils. In the context of a topic on food, the importance of soil as a growing medium could be linked to problems of food supply in the Third World.

A number of investigations into soils rely upon the use and application of a variety of mathematical skills and concepts particularly within Attainment Target 8.
- Observing and recording the water content of soils in terms of shrinkage and loss of weight.
- Observing and recording the composition of soils.
- Investigating the ability of various soils to soak up water.
- Investigating the extent to which various soils hold water or allow it to drain away.
- Investigating how resistant various soils are to wind erosion.
- Investigating how successful various soils are as a growing medium for a number of plants.

Adopt ways of measuring which are at a suitable level for the children. For example, while children are expected to be able to use grams as a measurement of mass, the litre as a measure for water is not specified until Level 4. Time could therefore be used as the measurement for soaking and drainage rates.

Essential language
Gram, centimetre, estimate, bar chart, values, axis, horizontal, vertical.

ATs 1AB, 8ABC, 9B, 13A.

PEDESTRIANS COUNTED IN THE HIGH STREET BETWEEN 10AM AND 10.15AM
OUTSIDE

Chemists	🥾 🥾 🥾 🥾 🥾 🥾
Church	🥾 🥾
Supermarket	🥾 🥾 🥾 🥾 🥾 🥾 🥾
Discount Centre	🥾 🥾 🥾 🥾

🥾 = 10 PEDESTRIANS   🥾 = less than 10 Passengers

Pavements

Roads and traffic are often investigated, but it is less common to carry out studies of pavements and the traffic which passes along them. The ideas outlined below involve the use and application of mathematical skills in order to produce useful information about the provision made for pedestrian traffic.

- How many pedestrians use a stretch of pavement within a given period of time?
- In which direction do most people go?
- Are some stretches of the same pavement busier than others?
- Are some pavements busier than others?
- Is the traffic along pavements fairly constant or are some times busier than others?
- How wide are pavements?
- Is there any correlation between the width of pavements and the amount of traffic they carry?

Close and careful supervision and assistance from adults will be required while the children are carrying out these activities.

As a result of collecting and presenting this sort of information the children will be able to infer whether pavements are adequate for the traffic they bear.

Essential language
Estimate, approximate, metre, centimetre, bar, chart, pictogram, axis, horizontal, vertical.

ATs 1AB, 2A, 3A, 8BC, 9ABC, 12AB, 13AB.

Shape sorting

At this level, children need to investigate the properties of two- and three-dimensional shapes in order to be able to sort such shapes in different ways and give reasons for each method of sorting.

Two-dimensional shapes

Using simple 'tick-off' recording sheets, encourage the children to investigate the following properties of two-dimensional shapes:
- The number of sides (edges).
- The number of corners (vertices).
- Whether the edges are straight or curved.
- Whether the edges are all the same length or not.
- Whether the vertices are the same size or not.
- The number of axes of reflective symmetry (this can be investigated by cutting out shapes and folding them along the axes of symmetry, or by using a mirror).

Include both regular and irregular shapes for the children to investigate.

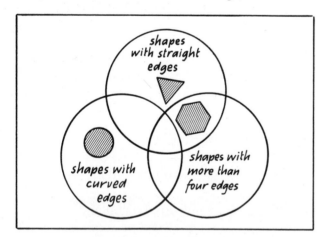

Three dimensional shapes

The same sort of recording sheet can be used when investigating the following properties of three-dimensional shapes:
- The number of faces.
- Whether the faces are flat or curved.
- The shape of each of the faces.
- The number of edges.
- Whether the edges are straight or curved.
- Whether the edges are the same length or not.

- The number of corners (vertices).

When investigating pyramids, further properties may be outlined:
- The shape of each face.
- The shape of the base.
- The number of base vertices.
- The total number of vertices.
- The number of base edges.
- The total number of edges.

Database of shapes

The children's findings could be recorded in a simple database, using fieldnames like those in the example below:

Name: cube
Number of faces: six
Shape of faces: square
Flat or curved faces?: flat
Number of edges: 12
Straight or curved edges?: straight
Number of vertices: eight

When completed, let the children use the database to sort the shapes. Try questions such as these:
- Which shapes have curved faces?
- Which shapes have more than six faces?
- Which shapes have both flat and curved faces?

Sorting activities

Shapes could be sorted in many different ways according to their properties, using intersecting set rings or logic gates. First the teacher and then the children could decide upon the properties of each set.

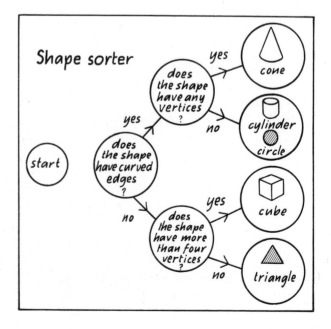

Such activities should provide the children with valuable experience of sorting two- and three-dimensional shapes in different ways.

Twenty questions

This game involves two children, one of whom thinks of a shape whilst the second asks questions about the properties of that shape in order to determine what it is.

The child who is answering may only reply 'yes' or 'no' to each question. The second child is allowed to ask a maximum of 20 questions, and scores points for correctly determining the shape within that limit. For example, if the child discovers the identity of the shape after nine questions, then he scores 11 points (the number of questions remaining).

Essential language

Side, edge, corner, vertex, straight, curved, axes of symmetry, reflective symmetry, face, base.

ATs 9BC, 10, 11A.

Function machines

As part of Attainment Target 6, children at this level are required to 'deal with inputs to and outputs from simple function machines'.

A 'function' in this case is simply a mathematical operation, such as 'add 4', which is performed on a succession of input numbers in order to produce a corresponding set of output numbers, the result of the operation.

Develop the children's use of function machines through the following suggested stages:

● Give the child both the input and the function, for the child to provide the output numbers.

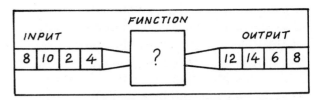

● Give the child the input numbers and output numbers, so that he or she can try to discover the function.

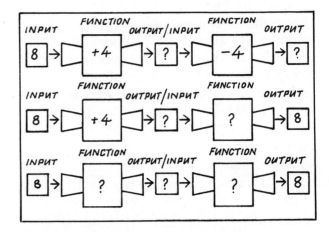

● Ask the children to operate two opposite function machines. This can help their understanding of inverse law.

Make a function machine

Introduce this work by making a large function machine from cardboard boxes and junk materials.

Let a child sit inside the 'machine' and perform a given function on numbers input by other children. The child inside the function machine is handed numbered cards by the others, and uses the set of cards inside the machine to produce the outputs, according to the particular function.

At a later stage the child could perform a mystery function for the other children to discover on the basis of the numbers in the input and output sets.

This kind of activity could be developed by asking the children to design and make their own function machines, either as an art and craft activity or as a design and technology project.

Essential language

Function, input, output, add, subtract, deduct, minus, take away, predict, multiply, divide.

ATs 3AC, 5AC, 6.

Multiples of two

These activities look at the properties of the multiples of two, although the same activities may be applied to the multiples of any number. They will help children increase their knowledge of multiplication tables, provide experiences in explaining number patterns and help them to recognise whole numbers which are divisible by two.

100 squares

The pattern made by multiples of two within a 100 square may be shown by colouring every second square, which reveals a pattern of alternate columns.

When the children have coloured the multiples of two, ask them to describe the pattern and list the first ten multiples of two.

1	2	3	4	5	6	7	8	9	10
11	12	13	14	15	16	17	18	19	20
21	22	23	24	25	26	27	28	29	30
31	32	33	34	35	36	37	38	39	40
41	42	43	44	45	46	47	48	49	50
51	52	53	54	55	56	57	58	59	60
61	62	63	64	65	66	67	68	69	70
71	72	73	74	75	76	77	78	79	80
81	82	83	84	85	86	87	88	89	90
91	92	93	94	95	96	97	98	99	100

At a later stage the multiples of two, four and eight could be coloured on the same 100 square, using a different colour for each set of multiples, in order to emphasise the relationship between these sets of multiples and to reveal the numbers they have in common.

Units digits

When the children have found the first ten multiples of two, ask them to list the units digit of each in order. This should reveal the following pattern: 2, 4, 6, 8, 0, 2, 4, 6, 8, 0.

Ask the children whether they can see a pattern in these units digits. Show the

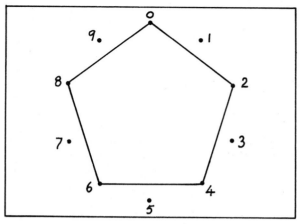

cyclical nature of the pattern by representing it on a ten-point circle, as shown.

Multiple graphs

Draw a bar chart to represent the multiples of two. A graph such as this is useful as it clearly shows the regular growth of multiples patterns.

After taking part in such activities the children should be able to recognise the whole numbers which are divisible by two as those which have an even number in the units place.

At this level children would be expected to perform similar activities with the multiples of five and of ten, and appreciate that any whole number which has a five or

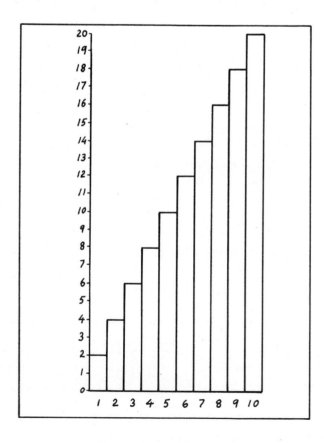

a zero in the units place will be divisible by five, and that any whole number with a zero in the units place will be divisible by ten.

Essential language
Multiples, pattern, alternate, common multiples, units, digit, cycle, divisible.

ATs 1BC, 3C, 5AC, 13A.

Using LOGO

At this level children who have access to floor turtles should be able to use LOGO to draw squares and rectangles; therefore they will know that the size of the angles in these shapes is 90°.

Using this knowledge the children could then be asked to turn the turtle from one given compass point to another, at first using the four cardinal points and then moving on to the eight points of the compass.

The children should deduce that the angle between each of the eight points is half of 90 degrees, or 45 degrees, and that the angle between any two of the eight points is a multiple of 45 degrees.

In drawing squares and rectangles the children will be inputting amounts into the computer in order to move or rotate the turtle. In doing this they will be doubling and halving, adding and subtracting, and when correcting errors they will come to realise that the correction is an inverse operation to the error.

Essential language
Input, output, angle, degrees, square, rectangle.

ATs 1ABC, 2A, 6, 9C, 11AB.

Place value games

The games described here provide an enjoyable way for children to develop their ability to read, write and order numbers up to 1000 and to use the knowledge that the position of a digit indicates its value.

UNITS	TENS	HUNDREDS

Game 1

This game may be played by any number of children, from two to a whole group.

What you need

For each child, a piece of paper with three boxes representing the hundreds, tens and units columns and a ten-sided die.

What to do

Each child in turn rolls the die three times. After each roll of the die the child must place the uppermost number into one of the three boxes in order to make the largest number possible.

When all the boxes have been filled, the player who has made the largest number is the winner.

The game may continue in this way, or the target may be changed for each round; for example the smallest possible number, a number between 400 and 600, and so on. The computer equivalent of this game is known as *Size Game*, and can be found in the MEP Primary Maths Pack.

Game 2

This is a slightly more complicated version of Game 1.

What you need
A series of boxes like those in Game 1, but set out as below; die.

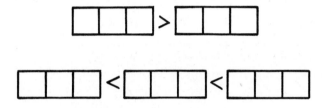

What to do
For this game, the aim is to place digits in the boxes in an order which will make the number sentences true. As before, the number of times the die is rolled by each player corresponds to the number of boxes, so each child gets a chance to fill all the boxes before scores are compared.

Points are scored according to how many of the numbers in each number sentence are in the correct order.

Game 3

This game is for four players.

What you need
Copies of the board as shown; die.

What to do
The die is rolled in turn by each of the children up to a total of twelve times. At his or her turn a player writes the number showing on the die into one of the boxes, but this time he or she has free choice of any box on the board, and so may choose to put low numbers in the other players' boxes.

PLAYER 1

PLAYER 2

PLAYER 3

PLAYER 4

When all the boxes have been filled, the player having the largest number scores four, the player with the next largest scores three, and so on.

There are many variations of this game, which adapts well whether played in groups or against a computer, and the children could also be encouraged to develop their own versions.

Essential language
Digit, hundred, ten, unit, position, value, column, order, sequence, more than, less than.

ATs 1AB, 2A, 4A.

Lines

This is a simple investigation in which the children make two rows of different numbers of dots, and then join each dot in one row to each dot in the other row, and count the resulting lines.

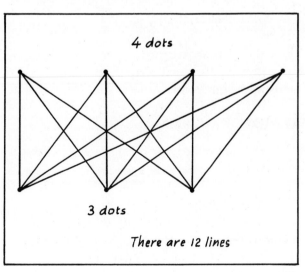

The aim of the investigation is to find a general rule or formula which connects the number of dots in the first row and the number of dots in the second row with the number of joining lines.

What you need
Pencil and paper for each child.

What to do
Ask the children to begin by drawing rows of dots and joining them. Advise them to try with just a few dots at first.

Encourage the children to tabulate their trials and results carefully.

1st set dots	2nd set dots	lines
4	3	12

As the children develop their tables of results, ask them to see if they can discover a relationship between the number of dots in each row and the number of joining lines.

The relationship in this case is quite an easy one; the number of joining lines may be found by multiplying the number of dots in one row by the number of dots in the other.

This investigation is also available as a computer program, also called *Lines*, in which the chosen number of dots are drawn and joined on the screen and the table of results is kept automatically. The *Lines* program is available from MUSE, PO Box 43, Hull HU1 2HD.

Essential language
Row, investigate, relationship, multiply, factors, products, pattern.

ATs 1BC, 3C, 5A, 9ABC.

Clocks

This is an investigation into the patterns made by adding the numbers on 'clock faces' of different sizes. For example, on a ten-clock, or a clock face divided into ten

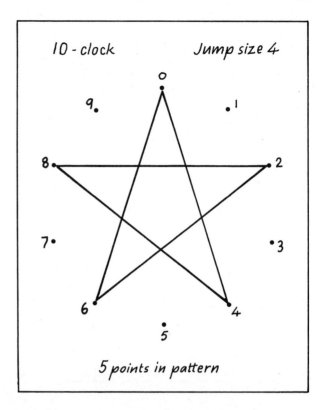

10 - clock   Jump size 4

5 points in pattern

sections, the numbers visited for addition in jumps of four would be nought, four, eight, two, six and back to nought. The number of points in the completed pattern would be five.

What you need
Sheets of 'clocks' with different number values.

What to do
Prepare sheets of 12-clocks for the children and ask them to find the number of points in completed patterns for jumps of three, five and eight. Then ask them to try jumps of other sizes.

Next, ask the children to look at the patterns made by different-sized jumps on clocks with various number values.

Divide the children into groups of four so that each group investigates clock faces of a different size.

Encourage the children to keep a careful record of their trials by completing a table.

As more examples are tried, ask the children to see if they can discover a relationship between the size of the clock, the size of the jump and the number of points in a complete pattern.

At this stage, gather the children together to pool the groups' results and share ideas.

The relationship here is that the number of points in a complete pattern is found by dividing the number of sections on the clock by the highest common factor of both the number of sections on the clock and the size of jump.

Number of sections on clock	Size of jump	Number of points
10	4	5
10	2	5

This investigation may also be carried out on a computer. There are at least two programs available, namely *Clocks* and *Circle*, which allow children to specify the number of sections on the clock and the size of jump, and display the resulting pattern, also keeping a table of results. *Clocks* is available from MUSE, PO Box 43, Hull HU1 2HD, and *Circle* from ILECC (SMILE), at 275 Kennington Lane, London SE11 5QZ.

Essential language
Points, count on, pattern, relationship, sections, highest common factor.

ATs 1AB, 3B, 5A, 11AB.

Heads or tails?

This activity introduces children to probability. It is concerned with the outcomes of repeated tosses of a single coin.

What you need
A coin for each group of children; paper and pencils for graphs and tallies.

What to do
Introduce the idea of probability by discussing the likelihood of certain events occurring. Ask the children whether, for example, the headteacher becoming prime minister or the bell ringing at the end of playtime are 'certain', 'likely', 'unlikely' or 'impossible'.

Discuss with the children the possible ways that a coin could fall if tossed. Ask them how many outcomes are possible when tossing a coin. At this point introduce the term 'evens' as a way of describing the chance of tossing either a head or a tail.

Ask the children to predict the number of heads and tails they would expect to score if they were to toss a coin ten times. Ask them to test their predictions, recording each toss of the coin on a tally chart and then representing the results by means of a bar chart.

Ask the children to compare results. Discuss what they notice about the different results, and whether they feel that ten tosses represents a fair sample.

Next ask the children to toss their coin 50 times, recording as before. Ask them to predict the number of 'heads' and 'tails' they expect to get this time.

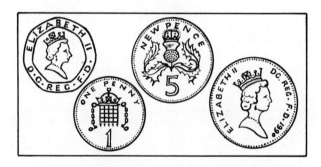

Once again, ask the children to compare results and discuss their findings in relation to their predictions. At this stage ask the children to combine their results and produce a bar chart which displays the combined results. When this is complete ask the children whether the combined results are closer to their prediction. Take the opportunity here to introduce the idea that the larger the sample, the more likely the results are to be close to the expected outcome.

Essential language
Likelihood, chance, certain, likely, unlikely, impossible, outcome, head, tail, evens, predict, fair sample, results.

ATs 13A, 14ABC.

Shape maker

'Shape maker' is an investigation which involves making different two-dimensional shapes on a pinboard with nine pins. The aim of the activity is to find all the different shapes which can be made on the pinboard, beginning with triangles.

What you need

For each pair of children, a pinboard with nine pins, an elastic band, a sheet of square dot lattice paper.

What to do

First, discuss with the children what is meant by the term 'different'; in this case we mean 'not congruent', although it is not necessary to introduce such terminology at this stage. All that is really necessary is to show the children two shapes side by side which they may consider to be different, although they are the same shape in a different orientation or position.

Once the idea of 'difference' has been established, the children can begin their investigation, using a sheet of square dot lattice paper to record their findings.

- Ask the children to try to find eight different triangles using the pinboard and elastic band. (Figure 1)

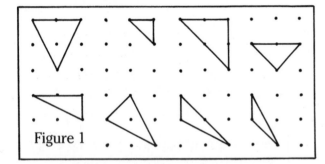

Figure 1

- The next stage of the activity involves the children in finding 16 different quadrilaterals. (Figure 2)

- Then the children can be asked to find 23 different pentagons. (Figure 3)

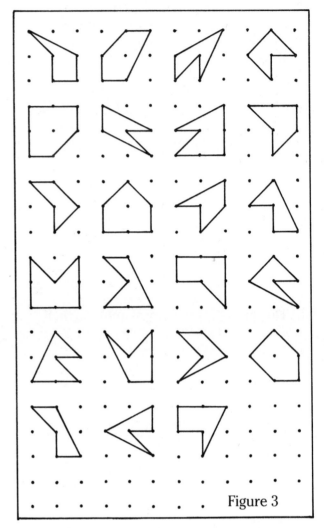

Figure 3

This investigation is also useful for dispelling the idea held by many children that, for example, the only pentagon is a regular pentagon. Instead children will see that any five-sided shape is a pentagon.

Essential language

'Different', triangle, quadrilateral, pentagon, regular, irregular.

ATs 9ABC, 10, 11A.

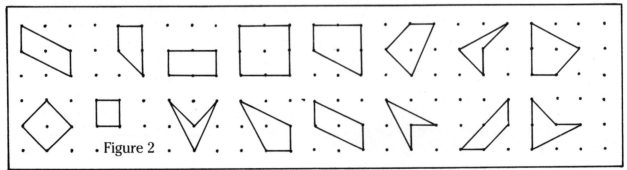

Figure 2

The symmetry game

This is a game for two players involving the development of patterns which possess reflective symmetry.

What you need

A pegboard and pegs (or coloured construction cubes and a 10 × 10 squared board), squared paper, coloured pencils or pens and a mirror. The board is divided into two halves by a line which indicates the axis of symmetry.

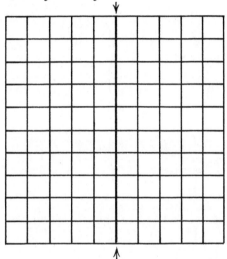

What to do

At the start of the game the first player places a coloured peg or cube anywhere on their half of the board. The second player then has to place a peg or cube of the same colour in the corresponding position on their half of the board, using the mirror to assist if necessary.

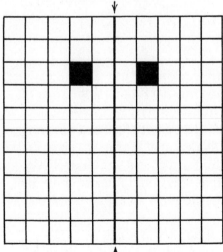

The players keep a record of each placing of a peg or cube by colouring the corresponding squares on their squared

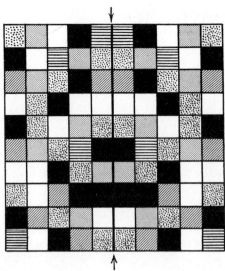

paper.

The second player then places a peg or cube in any position on their half of the board; the first player then has to mimic that move by placing a peg or cube of the same colour in the corresponding position on their half of the board. The game continues in this way until the board is full, resulting in a pattern of squares which possesses bilateral symmetry.

Essential language

Axis of symmetry, reflective symmetry, reflect, reflection, position, half.

ATs 9B, 11A.

Tile designs

This is an art activity in which children use reflective symmetry to produce designs for square tiles which will have two axes of symmetry.

What you need

A supply of art paper, tracing paper, pencils and paints or fibre-tipped pens.

What to do

Begin by drawing a square of, say, 30cm, which is then divided into quarters. Some straight or curved lines are then drawn in the top left-hand quarter, as shown.

The resulting design is traced on to a square of tracing paper which is then turned (flipped) over on the vertical axis in order to transfer the reflection of the design onto the top right-hand quarter, as shown on the next page.

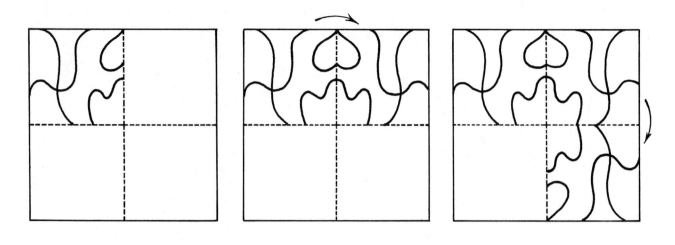

The next stage is to slip over the tracing on the horizontal axis in order to transfer the reflection of the design onto the bottom right-hand quarter, and then flip it over to the bottom left-hand corner, so completing the design of the tile. The resulting tile may then be coloured in to display its symmetry.

The tile design can then be repeated to give the impression of a tiled surface, creating new patterns where the individual tiles join.

In taking part in this activity, the children will get direct experience of reflective symmetry.

Take the activity further by making clay tiles. Mark a symmetrical design on the tiles, and use glazes to colour it. The resulting tiles could then be mounted together to form an attractive mural.

Essential language

Axes of symmetry, reflect, 'flip over', repeat, vertical/horizontal axis, quarter.

ATs 9B, 11A.

North American Indian art

A study of the North American Indians would link in well with a number of topics; it also contains elements of many aspects of the curriculum, including geography, world history, religious education, English and the expressive arts.

This topic also provides an excellent context in which to develop children's ideas of geometric patterns and, in particular, their understanding of reflective symmetry.

The Plains Indian tribes, such as the Sioux and the Cheyenne, decorated their clothing and other belongings with colourful geometric designs which were nearly always symmetrical. Before the advent of Europeans the patterns were sewn or plaited using dyed and flattened porcupine quills, but the Europeans traded coloured glass beads with the Indians and these were sewn on to produce the well-known Indian beadwork embroidery.

Completing patterns

Geometric designs like the traditional American Indian ones may be used to form a basis for the investigation and development of symmetrical geometric patterns.

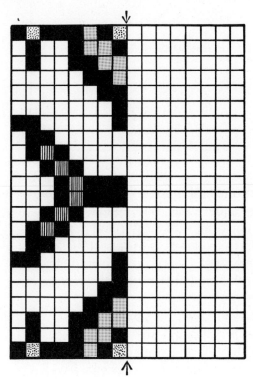

What you need

Cards showing half an Indian pattern for each child; squared paper, coloured pencils.

What to do

Let the children copy the half-patterns that appear on the cards on to a piece of 1cm squared paper, and then complete the pattern by drawing the reflection of the half-pattern on to the other half of the paper. A mirror may help in determining the reflection of the half-pattern.

Designing patterns

The Plains Indians used large geometric designs for the decoration of larger articles, such as breechcloths, gauntlets and rawhide folders for storing clothing. Encourage the children to design their own large patterns.

What you need

Square dot lattice paper or squared paper, coloured pencils, ruler.

What to do

To create a design, outline a square with sides of 16cm, and then divide it into four equal quarters by drawing the horizontal and vertical axes of symmetry.

The next stage is to draw a design in one of the quarters by joining dots (or the corners of squares) with straight lines.

In order to complete the pattern symmetrically, this design is first reflected in the vertical axis and then in the horizontal axis.

The completed designs could then be used as a basis for appliqué work.

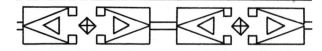

Variations

Headbands and shirts were often decorated with thin strips of beadwork which contained a repeated symmetrical pattern. The children could design their own border patterns using long strips of 5mm squared paper.

The children's designs could then be used to make items of beadwork, sewing coloured glass beads on to woven fabric, or by weaving the beads on a bead loom.

Other ways of representing Indian designs include collage, sewing on binca, weaving with strips of paper or with wool, and mosaics.

Essential language

Symmetry, symmetrical, geometric, design, axes of symmetry, horizontal, vertical, reflect.

ATs 11A.

Rangoli patterns

During Diwali, the Festival of Lights, Hindus make traditional geometric patterns on the ground, often on doorsteps or areas just outside the door. These patterns are known as Rangoli patterns and are used to welcome guests into the house.

The patterns are usually made using rice powder, rice paste and coloured chalk. Rangoli patterns are usually symmetrical, but not always.

Symmetrical Rangoli patterns can be created on paper by the children.

What you need

Square dot lattice paper, rulers, pencils, mirrors, colouring materials.

What to do

First, ask the children to outline a 9 × 9 array of dots in which to draw their pattern.

Next they can draw vertical and horizontal axes of symmetry, dividing the square into quarters, and then draw a diagonal axis of symmetry in the top left-hand quarter.

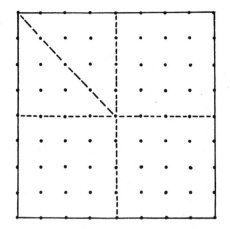

In one half of the top left-hand quarter of their square the children can draw lines by joining dots with a ruler and pencil.

The next stage is to reflect these lines along the diagonal axis of symmetry, so that the top left-hand square is entirely filled in.

Then reflect the pattern vertically, using a mirror to help if necessary.

The pattern is then completed by reflecting along the horizontal axis.

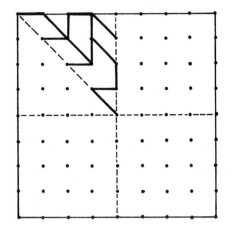

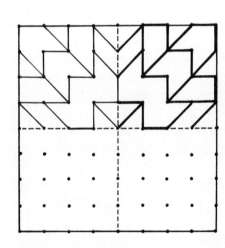

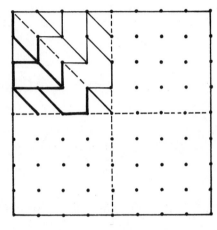

The final stage is for the children to colour the patterns in a way which displays the symmetry.

The resulting designs make an attractive display which could be combined with a display of other aspects of the Diwali festival.

Essential language
Symmetrical, axes of symmetry, vertical, horizontal, diagonal, reflect.

ATs 9B, 11A.

Moving shadows

Using shadows cast by the sun is one of the oldest (if in our temperate climate most uncertain) means of telling the time. To anyone without access to clocks it would, climate permitting, remain a useful way of telling the time.

What you need
A shadow stick approximately two metres high.

What to do
Place the stick in a sunny location. The children can take readings at intervals during the day, noting changes in the length and direction of the shadow.

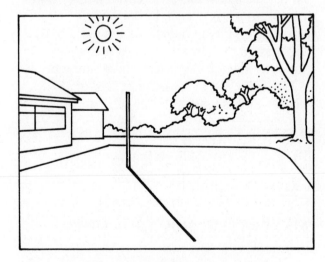

Encourage the children to discuss the best way of recording these measurements so that any patterns in the results become clear. Consider for example the time when the shortest shadow was cast, and the direction in which this shadow pointed.

Take the same measurements one day each week or month, and note the recurring similarities and differences. To simplify comparisons, just the length and direction of midday shadows could be taken.

In undertaking such a study children will be exercising measuring skills, making and using tables and lists, and constructing and interpreting bar charts. Importantly it provides an ideal context for the use and application of mathematics. At the same time the science statements of attainment at this level within Attainment Target 16 will be addressed.

Essential language
The eight points of the compass, centimetre, bar chart, value, axis, horizontal, vertical.

ATs 1ABC, 8ABC, 9ABC, 11B, 12AB, 13A.

Cooking

Cooking provides an exciting context for experience of measuring. Cooking can enhance any topic on food, and it can also give an insight into other cultures and countries, and the choice or lack of choice of food which people from various parts of the world have. You can also use cooking to highlight the importance of a balanced diet.

These simple recipes can be used to address these issues while fulfilling the appropriate science statements of attainment.

The recipes for Scotch shortbread and potato fingers were recommended during the Second World War as an economical means of providing energy and bulk at a time of shortages and constraint.

Kulfi

What you need
Two 410g tins of evaporated milk
100g ground almonds
Six 15ml spoons caster sugar
Half tsp vanilla essence

What to do
● Whisk the ingredients.
● Pour the mixture into a plastic freezer container.
● Freeze overnight.
● Cut into slices and serve.

Roti

What you need
450g wholemeal flour
Half tsp salt
250–300 ml water
A small amount of fat for frying

What to do
- Sieve the flour and salt into a bowl.
- Gradually add the water and mix to a soft dough.
- Cover and leave for five minutes.
- Divide the dough into 25g balls.
- Roll each into a thin circle about 15cm in diameter.
- Lightly grease a thick-bottomed frying pan, and warm over a medium heat.
- When the pan is hot, place the first of the shaped roti on to it.
- Turn the roti over to prevent burning (don't worry if they puff up but be wary of jets of escaping hot air).
- Cover and keep warm before eating as they are, or spread with butter or ghee.

Finnish biscuits

What you need
150g plain flour
75g brown sugar
100g margarine
Half tsp almond essence

What to do
- Cream the sugar and margarine, and stir in the flour. Add the almond essence.
- Mix together well, and knead to a smooth dough.
- Roll out thinly.
- Cut into shapes.
- Place on a greased baking tray, and bake at 130° C for 25–30 minutes.

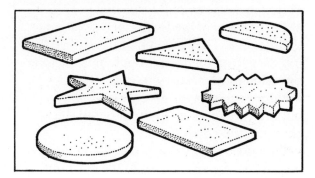

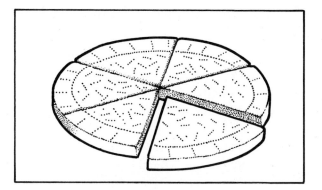

Scotch shortbread

What you need
100g margarine
200g plain flour
50g sugar

What to do
- Melt the margarine.
- Add the flour and sugar and mix well.
- Knead the mixture until it binds together.
- Place the mixture onto an ungreased shallow cake tin and press down to make a 1.5cm thick round.
- Prick with a fork and score lightly into segments, then bake in the centre of a moderate oven for about 20 minutes.

Potato fingers

What you need
200g mashed potato
25g plain flour
Milk to mix
Salt and pepper to taste
Egg (optional)

What to do
- Mix the mashed potato and flour.
- Season with salt and pepper and if necessary bind with a little milk.
- Shape the mixture into fingers.
- If desired glaze with beaten egg or milk.
- Bake in a hot oven for ten minutes.

Essential language
Gram, approximately, increase, deduct, balance pan, scales, digital scales, display, dial.

ATs 1A, 4A, 8ABC.

Escape from Planet X

Children at this level are now required to appreciate the meaning of negative whole numbers in familiar contexts. Games such as this will familiarise them with moving along a positive/negative whole number line in the context of temperature

This game can be played by any number of players.

What you need
One large game board (see photocopiable page 182); a token for each player; a pack of cards prepared by the teacher (see illustration).

What to do
The players are asked to imagine that they have landed in their spacecraft on Planet X.

This planet is renowned throughout the galaxy for its abrupt fluctuations in temperature. On landing the temperature is that shown on the starting position on the board. At this temperature a certain vine-like form of plant life is at its most virulent, and it immediately seizes the landing gear of the spacecraft in a vice-like grip. The intrepid adventurers are marooned on the planet!

All is not lost, however, because as the temperature goes down the rogue plant recedes into a dormant state, so by the time the bottom of the board is reached the plant has relaxed its grip and released the stranded spacecraft.

At the start of the game the players place tokens representing their spacecraft on the starting position of the board. Players move by taking turns to pick up the top card from the pack which the teacher has prepared in advance, and moving their token the number of spaces shown.

The cards should have mostly negative values, so that all players will gradually move downwards.

The winner of the game will be the first to escape from the clutches of the plant and leave the planet in safety.

Essential language
Negative, positive, Celsius, degrees, temperature, plus, minus.

ATs 2C, 3A.

Spanish Main

This game will provide up to four children with ample opportunities to add and subtract numbers from one to twenty. It also gives practice in using the points of the compass, and in planning a strategy for the game in advance.

The aim of the game is to get to the island at the centre of the board.

What you need
A board as shown, a calculator, and a pack of 20 or so cards to indicate wind direction.

What to do
Players select one of the starting positions at the corners of the board, and position their tokens. They take turns to remove the top card from the pack, which indicates the direction in which they have to move. Initially each player will only have the opportunity to move in three out of the eight possible directions.

If the move shown is possible, the player can move one space only in the direction

8	16	7	14	3	6	15	4	13	8
2	11	20	4	9	10	2	15	20	5
6	20	8	6	10	5	9	4	9	16
16	12	16	12	4	15	18	6	12	3
6	20	5	8	17	27	16	20	2	13
11	16	7	13	15	20	6	19	4	11
17	10	15	6	4	4	10	13	1	16
2	7	2	11	16	9	2	18	9	11
18	15	8	18	2	12	7	8	17	3
8	4	16	6	9	7	18	6	12	8

indicated by the card. To move, enter into the calculator the number of the space presently occupied, and add or subtract an amount which will increase or reduce this to the number in the adjacent space. A move can only follow a correct answer.

Once a player's token has moved in from the fringe of the board, he can choose a route to the island. If the wind direction card turned over would take a player in the wrong direction, he can stay put and wait for a more favourable wind. To do this he must calculate the difference between the number in the space presently occupied

and that in the space into which the wind is blowing him. If the answer is right, he can stay where he is; if wrong, he has to move. The winner is the first player to guide his or her ship to the island.

Back up this activity with the computer game *Spanish Main*, by Tecmedia, from the MEP Microprimer Pack 3.

Essential language
Eight points of the compass, add, increase, take away, subtract, deduct, minus.

ATs 3AC, 6, 11B.

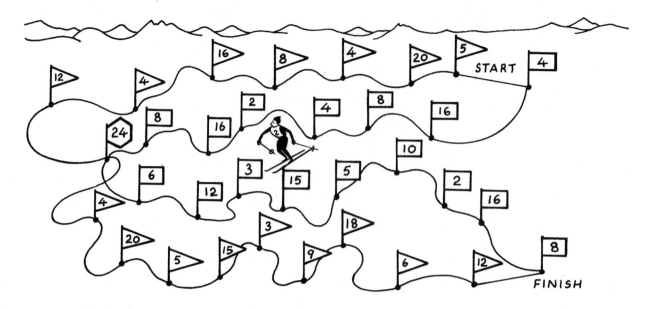

Downhill run

As they progress along the number track in this game, children must supply factors or divisors, which gives an opportunity for learning and practising the number facts specified at this level. 'Downhill run' is a game for two to four children.

What you need
A board as shown (see also photocopiable page 183), a calculator, tokens, a coin.

What to do
Players select a starting point for their downhill run and position their tokens.

The toss of a coin decides who is the first away from the start, and the winner of the toss enters the starting number into the calculator.

To move down the slope to the next number, the multiply or divide key must be used along with a number key to produce the number on the next flag.

An incorrect answer means that the skier must wait and attempt the same move the next time.

Players take turns to move except when crossing points are reached. Make up your own rules to govern what happens when players land here.

The first to the bottom of the slope is the winner.

Teachers will no doubt think of a number of alternative race boards, some of which could be used to give practise with specific multiplication tables.

A similar game could be used to give practice with remainders and rounding up or down. In this case, in order to move, the factor which provides the answer closest to the target number must be given in order for a token to continue on its downhill run.

Essential language
Factor, product, quotient, dividend, divisor, remainder.

ATs 3BC, 4B, 5C, 6.

Ergo

Ergo, a computer program supplied in the MEP Microprimer 3 pack, is still a worthwhile program to use with children at this level. It provides experience in explaining number patterns, and encourages the prediction of subsequent numbers.

What you need
Access to a computer and the *Ergo* program.

What to do
In *Ergo* the computer selects 25 numbers and arranges them in a particular order in a five by five square. At the start of the activity only two numbers are shown; the child is asked to guess the other numbers in the pattern.

After making a guess, the child is told

```
 ?     ?     ?     ?     ?

 ?     ?    ┌────┐  ?     ?
            │ 18 │
            └────┘
 ?     ?     ?     ?     ?

 ?     ?     ?     ?     ?

                        ┌────┐
 ?     ?     ?     ?    │ 25 │
                        └────┘
```
A typical Ergo screen display

whether this is correct or not.

If incorrect the player has the option of trying again or moving to another position on the screen by using the cursor keys. Extra points are scored for getting numbers right first time.

Essential language
Pattern, sequence, predict.

ATs 1BC, 3AC, 5A.

Hexangle

This game for two players aims to provide children with opportunities to find number patterns and equivalent forms of two-digit numbers and use these to perform mental calculations.

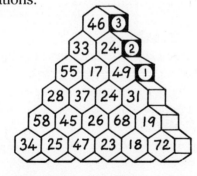

The object of the game is to move counters upwards to occupy the top six hexagons of the board. The game is won by the player who scores most points.

What you need
A board as shown (see photocopiable page 184), a calculator and three counters for each player.

What to do
The children place their counters in alternate spaces at the foot of the board. Once the game has commenced players may move their counters diagonally upwards or horizontally (but not downwards) to an adjoining hexagon.

To move a counter, a player enters into the calculator the number on which one of her counters is sitting, presses the plus key and then enters the number on the hexagon to which she wishes to move. She then has to add these two numbers mentally and state the total to her opponent, before checking the calculation.

If correct, the counter can be moved. If not, it has to remain where it is while the other player has a turn. Play continues in this way until the upper six hexagons are filled. Then the total score for each player is added up; the points awarded for attaining the top six spaces are shown alongside the spaces.

Children should be encouraged to use a number of strategies for adding two-digit numbers and recording their methods.

Essential language
Horizontally, diagonally, add, total.

ATs 1AB, 5B.

First number	Second number	Addition sentence	Calculation	Player's answer	Calculator's answer
47	45	47 + 45	47 + 3 + 45 - 3 50 + 42	92	92
45	28	45 + 28	40 + 5 + 20 + 8 60 + 13	93	93
34	58	34 + 58	34 + 60 - 2 94 - 2	92	92
28	55	28 + 55	20 + 50 + 13 70 + 13	83	83
58	28	58 + 28	58 + 20 + 8		

Level 3 glossary of terms

The following glossary explains some of the mathematical terms which are contained within the statements of attainment for mathematics at Level 3.

Approximate
To write a number or quantity as a value which is 'near enough'. The number 43 approximated to the nearest 10 is written 40.

Equivalent
Of equal value; eg 42+38 is equivalent to 42+40−2.

Function machine
An imaginary machine which obeys instructions, such as 'add 4', and carries out this operation on input numbers in order to produce output numbers.

Input
Data, in this case numbers, which are fed into a calculator or computer.

Inverse
Opposite; for example, addition is the inverse or opposite of subtraction: 10+4= 14 and 14−4=10.

Mental calculations
Arithmetic performed 'in the head', without recourse to pencil and paper or a calculator.

Output
Information which is fed out from a calculator or computer after some operation has been performed upon the input.

Reflective symmetry
Also referred to as bilateral or mirror symmetry. In a shape which possesses reflective symmetry each half of the shape is a mirror image of the other. The 'mirror line' is known as the axis of symmetry.

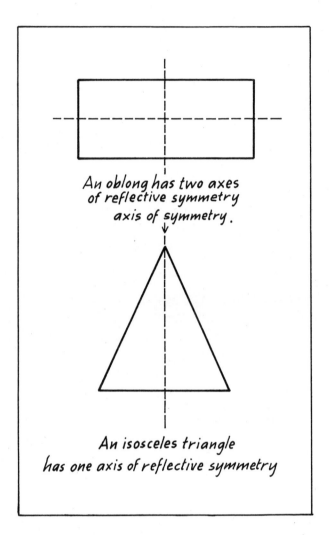

An oblong has two axes of reflective symmetry

axis of symmetry.

An isosceles triangle has one axis of reflective symmetry

Simple database
A computer program designed specifically for the storage of information, which should be easy for children to use.

Systematically
In an organised, ordered, methodical and logical way.

Round up/down
To round a number up or down we express it to a stated degree of accuracy; for example, when rounding to the nearest 10 the number is rounded to the nearest multiple of ten which is above or below it, whichever is the nearer; thus 88 would be rounded up to 90, whereas 84 would be rounded down to 80.

Level 3: Programme of Study

This diagram shows how the programme of study can be expanded, suggesting teaching stages where applicable.

- Represent numbers to 1000 using Multibase, abacuses and extended notation.
- Use the symbols < and > to order pairs of numbers.
- Arrange numbers in ascending and descending order.
- Represent numbers verbally and numerically.
- Understand the value of each digit.

- Count down and record numbers on a vertical number line which ends at zero, and on a number line which extends below zero.
- Appreciate that in science −3° is read as minus three degrees, and in maths −3 is read as negative three and +3 as positive three.
- Record negative calculator outputs on a vertical number line.
- Read temperatures on a thermometer.
- Construct graphs displaying temperatures below freezing point.

Multiplication:
- Understand the concept of 'sets of', and set notation; four sets of two is 4(2).
- Understand multiplication as repeated addition.
- Use the × sign: 4(2) is the same as 2 × 4.
- Understand that multiplication is commutative.
- Understand the distributive law for multiplication, eg. $15 \times 5 = (10 \times 5) + (5 \times 5)$.
- Multiply by multiples of ten.
- Multiply with whole numbers and money, first two-digit, then three-digit numbers, using extended and conventional notation.
- Approximate numbers to the nearest ten or 100 – useful for checking answers.

- Use extended notation to demonstrate the value of each digit.
- Arrange numbers in ascending and descending orders.
- Round up or down to the nearest ten or 100 on a number line or in measurement.

Using and applying mathematics
- Select the materials and the mathematics to use for a task.
- Check results, considering whether they are sensible.
- Explain work and record findings systematically.
- Make and test predictions.

Number
- Read, write and order numbers to at least 1000, and use the knowledge that the position of a digit indicates its value.
- Use decimal notation in recording money.
- Appreciate the meaning of negative whole numbers in familiar contexts.
- Know and use addition and subtraction facts to 20 (including zero).
- Solve problems involving multiplication or division of whole numbers or money, using a calculator where necessary.
- Know and use multiplication facts up to 5 × 5 and all those in 2, 5 and 10 multiplication tables.
- Recognise the first digit is the most important in indicating the size of a number and approximate to the nearest 10 or 100.
- Understand remainders and know whether to round up or down.

- Record money on a decimal abacus.
- Record money in column form.
- Record money in decimal form, where the decimal point separates the whole units from the parts of a unit.

- Learn addition and subtraction facts to 20 by various approaches.
- Use addition and subtraction facts in everyday situations.
- Show patterns in addition on a 100 square.
- Add tens and units with and without exchange, by both extended and conventional notation.
- Subtract two-digit numbers with and without decomposition, by both extended and conventional notation.

Division:
- Understand the partitive aspect of division and its use in measuring.
- Understand that multiplication and division are inverse operations.
- Identify factors belonging to equations whose answers are exact products.
- Divide using repeated subtraction.
- Identify the factors of equations whose two-digit answers are not exact products.
- Introduce remainders.
- Divide two-digit numbers by a single digit using extended notation.
Money:
- Recognise the different coins.
- Make up amounts and give change.
- Multiply and divide with sums of money less and greater than £1.

- Understand about multiplication arrangements and arrays.
- Know about products and factors.
- Use a multiplication square.
- Understand the patterns in multiplication tables.
- Practise and memorise multiplication facts.
- Know about square numbers.

Level 3: Programme of Study (continued)

- Make number patterns.
- Explore square numbers, triangular numbers and the Fibonacci sequence.

Weight:
- Understand the conservation of weight.
- Use half and quarter kilograms as measures.
- Weigh using 100g, 50g, 20g and 10g weights, both individually and in combination.
Time:
- Tell the time using the terms 'o'clock', 'half past', 'quarter past' and 'quarter to'.
- Use five minute intervals to tell the time.
- Start to use the 24 hour clock.
- Start to use the digital clock.
- Relate a digital display to a clock face.
- Calculate the passage of time in hours and minutes.

- Understand about right- and left-hand turns, and whole, half and quarter turns.
- Understand the terms 'clockwise' and 'anticlockwise'.
- Travel in different directions according to the four cardinal points of the compass.
- Rotate clockwise and anticlockwise to arrive at the four cardinal points.
- Recognise eight points of the compass.
- Use weather vanes, and apply compass directions to everyday situations.

Algebra
- Find number patterns and equivalent forms of two-digit numbers and use these to perform mental calculations.
- Explain number patterns and predict subsequent numbers.
- Recognise whole numbers divisible by 2, 5 and 10.
- Deal with inputs to and outputs from simple function machines.

Measures
- Use a wider range of metric units.
- Choose and use appropriate units and instruments; interpret numbers on a range of measuring instruments.
- Make estimates based on familiar units.

Shape and space
- Sort two- and three-dimensional shapes and give reasons.
- Recognise reflective symmetry in a variety of shapes in two and three dimensions.
- Use and understand compass bearings and the terms 'clockwise' and 'anticlockwise'.

Handling data
- Extract information from tables and lists.
- Enter and access information in a simple database.
- Construct and interpret bar charts and graphs (pictograms) where the symbol represents a group of units.
- Place events in order of 'likelihood' and use appropriate words to identify the chance.
- Understand the idea of 'evens'.
- Distinguish 'fair' and 'unfair'.

Length:
- Use the decimetre and centimetre.
- Estimate and measure in metres and centimetres – length, perimeter and circumference.
- Record measurements in decimal notation.
- Use a tape measure.
- Find perimeters without measuring.
- Find area by covering surfaces, by tessellation and by counting squares.
Capacity:
- Use the litre as a unit of capacity.
- Estimate and compare using half and quarter litre measures.

- Sort two-dimensional shapes by properties such as number, regularity and length of sides, and size of angles.
- Investigate shapes which tessellate.
- Sort three-dimensional shapes by properties such as number and shape of faces, number and length of edges, number and size of vertices.
- Investigate whether shapes roll and slide.

- Experiment with reflective symmetry by cutting and folding shapes, using a mirror and drawing along lines of symmetry.
- Investigate two- and three-dimensional shapes for reflective symmetry.
- Recognise axes of symmetry in pictures and objects.

Level 3 : attainment targets 1–6

Use this chart to check which attainment targets are covered by each activity.

ACTIVITY	1 A	1 B	1 C	2 A	2 B	2 C	3 A	3 B	3 C	4 A	4 B	5 A	5 B	5 C	6
Journey to school	●	●	●	●											
League tables						▲	●								
Party time	●	●	●		●			▲	●		▲				
Food prices					●										
Daily routines															
Weather records	●	●	●												
Investigating soils	●	●													
Pavements	●	●		●			●								
Shape sorting															
Function machines							●		●			●		●	▲
Multiples of two		●	●						●			●		●	
Using LOGO	●	●	●	●											▲
Place value games	●	●		▲					▲						
Lines		●	●						●			●			
Clocks		●	●					●			▲				
Heads or tails?															
Shape maker															
The symmetry game															
Tile designs															
North American Indian art															
Rangoli patterns															
Moving shadows	●	●	●												
Cooking	●								●						
Escape from Planet X						▲	●		●						
Spanish Main							▲		●						●
Downhill run								●	▲	●				●	●
Ergo		●	●				●		●		▲				
Hexangle	●	●											▲		

Key: ● = touches on
▲ = especially relevant

Level 3 : attainment targets 8–14

Use this chart to check which attainment targets are covered by each activity.
(There is no Attainment Target 7 at Level 3.)

ACTIVITY	8 A	8 B	8 C	9 A	9 B	9 C	10	11 A	11 B	12 A	12 B	13 A	13 B	14 A	14 B	14 C
Journey to school	•	•	•						•	•	•	•	•			
League tables																
Party time	•	•	•	•	•	•				•		•	•			
Food prices										•	▲					
Daily routines				•	•	•				•	•	•	•			
Weather records	•	•		•	•	•			•	▲	▲	•	•			
Investigating soils	•	▲	•	•								•				
Pavements		•	▲	•	•	•				•	•	•	•			
Shape sorting					•	•	▲	•								
Function machines																
Multiples of two												•				
Using LOGO						•		•	•							
Place value games																
Lines				•	•	•										
Clocks								•	•							
Heads or tails?												•		▲	▲	
Shape maker				•	•	•	▲	•								
The symmetry game					•			▲								
Tile designs					•			▲								
North American Indian art								▲								
Rangoli patterns					•			▲								
Moving shadows	•	•	•	•	•	•			▲	•	•	•				
Cooking	▲	▲	•													
Escape from Planet X																
Spanish Main										•						
Downhill run																
Ergo																
Hexangle																

Key: • = touches on
▲ = especially
relevant

Level 3 : Contexts

This chart shows the wider contexts of each activity.

ACTIVITY	Everyday situations	Everyday problems	Games and fun	Maths problems	Maths investigations	Calculator activities	Computer activities	English (Core)	Science (Core)	Art	PE	History	Geography	Music	Technology	Local Curriculum	RE	Possible topic link	School-wide themes
Journey to school	●	●											●			●		●	●
League tables			●								●								
Party time	●	●																●	●
Food prices	●					●		●										●	●
Daily routines	●															●		●	
Weather records	●					●			●				●		●			●	
Investigating soils									●									●	
Pavements	●	●											●			●		●	●
Shape sorting					●														
Function machines			●		●					●					●				
Multiples of two					●														
Using LOGO							●												
Place value games			●		●		●												
Lines					●		●												
Clocks					●		●												
Heads or tails?			●		●														
Shape maker				●															
The symmetry game			●		●														
Tile designs			●							●									
North American Indian art										●		●	●			●		●	
Rangoli patterns										●		●	●			●	●	●	
Moving shadows									●			●	●		●			●	
Cooking									●							●		●	●
Escape from Planet X			●			●		●											
Spanish Main			●			●		●					●					●	
Downhill run			●			●													
Ergo				●															
Hexangle			●			●													

Chapter four
Level 4

Introduction

Mathematics is a valuable tool which can be used to help solve real problems. Children at Level 4 will enjoy having the chance to work out the most efficient ways of tackling questions to do with energy conservation and the ways we can help protect our environment. They can also learn a great deal from applying mathematics to the organisation of events such as a sports day or school disco.

This chapter contains suggestions for activities to give children experience in creating decision tree diagrams. Activities are suggested which can help them begin to apply logic to their methods of testing structures and materials. They can also gain from exploring various ways of measuring, using a range of different measures.

Children can get a good deal of enjoyment and satisfaction from activities designed to help them see the meanings behind number patterns. At this level they will be exploring more complicated number patterns and learning how to express in words the geometrical and numerical relationships which they discover.

Energy

Energy is a highly topical and relevant contemporary issue, and many upper junior children will have at least a rudimentary awareness of conservation.

Both environmental and financial considerations mean that more and more schools are attempting to meet realistic targets for energy consumption. Involving the children in this will be a better and more lasting way of influencing their attitudes towards energy consumption than merely insisting on their closing doors and windows and switching off lights.

There are a number of activities which provide useful experiences, demanding the use of mathematical skills and testing understanding.

• Take indoor and outdoor temperatures and compare and correlate them.

• Take and compare temperatures in classrooms which receive a good deal of direct sunlight and those which do not.

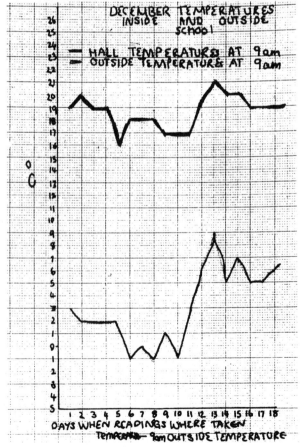

106

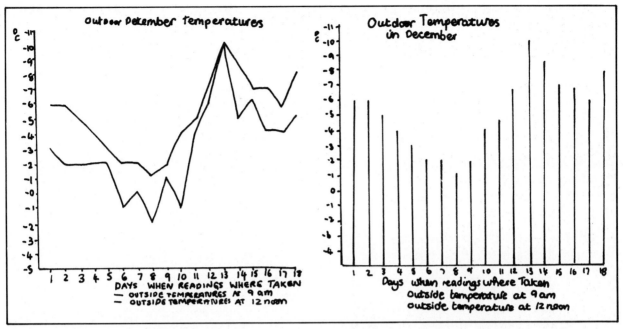

- Find warmer and cooler areas within classrooms.
- Compare temperatures within a room at different times of the day.
- Take and record maximum and minimum temperatures both indoors and outdoors, plotting the range between the two on a graph.
- Construct and interpret a frequency diagram, selecting suitable intervals for

temperature readings both indoors and outdoors.
- Take and record meter readings. Compare monthly meter readings, and calculate the mean and range of a set of data.
- Use meter readings to construct a frequency diagram, choosing suitable intervals covering the range for a discrete variable.
- Correlate energy consumption with external temperatures and weather conditions.
- Enter information into a database.
- Use information entered into a database over the past year to make comparisons and calculate the mean and range of a set of data.
- Investigate the effect of various appliances within the school on electricity consumption.
- Instigate economy drives and monitor their success.
- Devise a way to monitor the effect of insulation.
- Present the findings and conclusions to an audience.

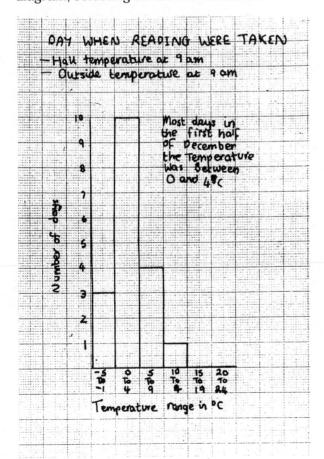

Essential language

Temperature, degrees, Celsius, maximum, minimum, comparison, correlate, mean, range, variable.

ATs 1ABC, 2ABCF, 3BC, 4ABC, 8AC, 9ABC, 12ABC, 13BCD.

107

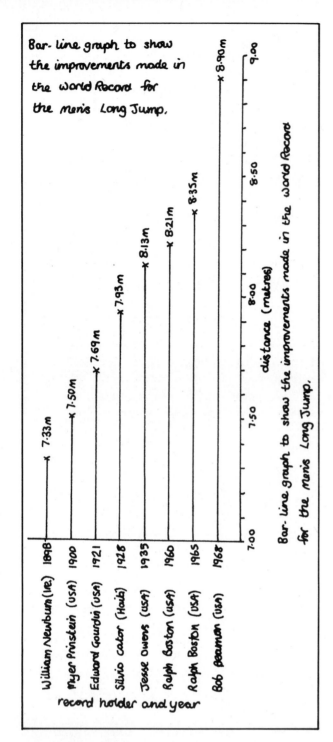

Bar-line graph to show the improvements made in the world Record for the men's Long Jump.

William Newburn (Ire.) 1898 — 7.33m
Myer Prinstein (USA) 1900 — 7.50m
Edward Gourdin (USA) 1921 — 7.69m
Silvio Cator (Haiti) 1928 — 7.93m
Jesse Owens (USA) 1935 — 8.13m
Ralph Boston (USA) 1960 — 8.21m
Ralph Boston (USA) 1965 — 8.35m
Bob Beamon (USA) 1968 — 8.90m

record holder and year

distance (metres)
7.00 7.50 8.00 8.50 9.00

Bar-line graph to show the improvements made in the world Record for the men's Long Jump.

Sports day

Sports day is a popular annual event in many schools. Rather than letting the whole burden of planning and organisation fall upon staff, try a new approach and involve the children in the design of their own sports day.

Children at this level could:
• Design races or activities.
• Draw up a programme of events.
• Organise equipment and apparatus.
• Apportion responsibilities for tasks such as marshalling, starting and judging.
• Devise a method of scoring, and ways of recording the scores.

In addition there is scope for work involving handling and presenting data:
• Timing or measuring events.
• Comparing performances, perhaps making allowances for age.
• Measuring the height and leg length of participants, to see whether such factors have any effect on performance.

Essential language
Time, minutes, seconds, tenths, hundredths, decimal point, length, measure, metres, centimetres, height, distance, bar-line graph.

ATs 1AB, 8AC, 9AB, 12ABC, 13BCD.

Disco

Children eagerly anticipate school social events such as discos. Very often the planning of such events is the exclusive province of a member of staff. Involving the children in planning will not necessarily reduce the burden placed upon staff, but it will make full use of a potentially motivating situation.

The planning of a school disco would involve the children in the following activities:
• Estimating the number of children who would be likely to attend (NB – consider fire safety requirements).
• Designing tickets (perhaps using symmetrical designs).
• Working out the costs involved in entertainment, refreshments, prizes, publicity and printing.
• Polling the opinions of likely attenders about the music to be played.
• Estimating, ordering and collecting refreshments.
• Deciding how much to charge, bearing costs in mind.

Essential language
Estimate, cost, survey, average.

ATs 1AB, 2BCDE, 3ABC, 4ABC, 9ABC, 12A, 13BCD.

Best buys

Does the local shop offer the best value for money, or could better value be obtained by going further afield? How does the range of goods sold at the local shop compare with those offered by larger competitors?

Children could investigate such ideas by undertaking a survey. First they could contact or visit local shops, and compare their prices for biscuits or soft drinks, for example. Such a survey would probably include the nearest local store and the largest store within the wider locality.

In making comparisons on the basis of price, children will need to subtract two-digit numbers mentally, and also subtract numbers with two decimal places. They could then add up some shopping bills, comparing the savings to be made by shopping at different stores. This would involve the mental addition of two-digit numbers as well as the addition of numbers with two decimal places.

In presenting their results children could calculate the mean price of certain items in order to establish more clearly any variance in price.

Essential language

Pounds, pence, compare, survey, best buy, grams, kilograms, millilitres, litres, estimate, approximate, round up, round down, mean, range, bar-line graph, values, axis, horizontal, vertical.

ATs 1ABC, 2ABCF, 3ABC, 4ABC, 9ABC, 12ABC, 13B.

Packaging

A visit to a local supermarket, store or even kitchen cupboard will reveal the variety of forms of packaging employed by manufacturers both to protect their products and to make them appeal to the buyer.

The children will use data handling skills in investigating various aspects of packaging.
- Which shapes are most commonly used, and why?
- Which materials are used most often,

and why?
- Which colours or combinations of colours are most popular, and why?
- How often is packaging really necessary? Why is it used in cases where it appears to be superfluous?
- What proportion of packaging is biodegradable?

Mathematics is being used here to increase awareness of the design process. Thinking about these issues may also help the children to arrive at some understanding of the relationship between consumer and product, and the environmental consequences of their interaction.

Sweet boxes

For Mothers' Day or another appropriate occasion children could make gifts such as toffee or fudge, and then be given the problem of designing a container for the sweets. This could involve constructing three-dimensional shapes from nets, which could then be decorated taking account of what had been learned from the surveys of packaging.

Similar containers could be used for investigations into volume; try filling them with cubes, unpacking them and counting the cubes.

Essential language

Centimetre, millimetre, net, prism, cube, pyramid, triangular, rectangular, hexagonal.

ATs 1A, 8ABC, 9ABC, 10B, 12AB, 13B.

Litter

The main purpose of tackling a real problem such as the issue of litter is to increase the children's concern for their environment. However, it can also involve the application of many mathematical skills.

Observation

Go with the children to look for litter along a main shopping street.

Investigate the situation, perhaps by organising a litter clear-up and recording the amount and type of litter produced.

The children will need to decide how the litter is to be counted, how many stops they will make to pick up litter, and the distance between the stops.

Clear-up

Ask the children to construct a plan of the route before the event. Show on the plan where the collection starts and finishes, and mark and number each stop. Locate the position of each of the litter bins, indicating possible litter problem areas.

A tally chart could be used during the collection, to record the sort of litter picked up. Children will have to estimate and approximate while they are counting the litter at each stop, and when assessing the total amount collected at the finish.

Analyse the litter into various groups, such as biodegradable/non-biodegradable, or recyclable/non-recyclable. This can involve percentages and fractions.

Throughout the project probability ranges will be explored, and the data accumulated can be represented on graphs. Try doing the activity at different times during the same day or at intervals

within a month. The mean can be calculated and the results compared.

Perhaps the children could telephone the local authority's Refuse Department to find out how often they collect litter in the area. The question can be posed alongside the children's findings – should the collections be made more frequently?

Essential language

Add, tally, total, estimate, approximate, measure, plan, scale, divide, decimal, fraction, equivalent, probability, average, mean, graph, calculate, rounding up, rounding down, nearest whole number.

ATs 1ABC, 2DE, 3BC, 4ABC, 8C, 9ABC, 12AB, 13BD, 14B.

Traffic survey

The problem of the increasing volume of traffic on our roads has become a major issue. Collecting information for a traffic survey provides children with opportunities to use and apply many mathematical skills. When surveying the traffic, look at the following areas:

- The amount of traffic at different times of day.
- The direction in which the traffic flows at various times of day.
- The type of traffic.
- Safe places to cross.
- Parking facilities. Would the painting of yellow lines on the road be an answer to any of the problems?
- Are there enough pedestrian crossings? If not, where should they be located?
- Where do most of the road accidents occur? Why might this be?

There may be other problems which are of particular concern in some areas. Involving the children in matters of this kind gives them the opportunity to take an active role in the control of their environment.

Essential language

Tally, total, average, mean.

ATs 12ABC, 13BD.

Buses

Look at local transport provision, and involve children in the use of timetables. A starting point for such an investigation could be the different ways of getting to school or into town, or planning a school journey. Ask the children to obtain the timetables themselves and use them to discover which buses would suit their purpose, when and how often is the service, and where they could board and alight from the bus.

This activity provides opportunities to use street maps, bus route maps, large scale Ordnance Survey maps and the children's own maps of routes.

Work on local transport could lead to:
- A comparison of the service offered by buses on different routes.
- Investigating the connection between fares and the length of journeys, which may reveal patterns which could be represented on graphs.
- Comparison of times taken for journeys on different routes, or on different sections of the same route.

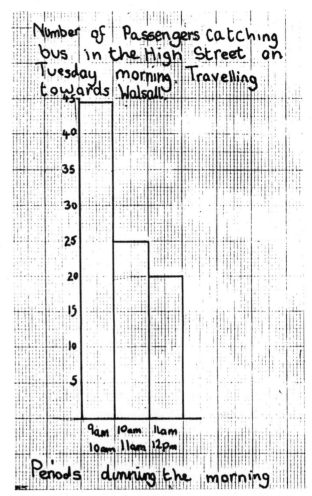

Number of Passengers catching bus in the High Street on Tuesday morning. Travelling towards Walsall.

Periods during the morning

Bus Services to Walsall from Bloxwich				*
Service	347	371	370	317
Depart Bloxwich	9.27	9.28	9.31	9.41
Arrive Walsall	9.57	9.55	9.44	10.13

* Leaves from Park Lane

- Comparing the regularity of the service with the number of passengers using it at different times of the day – is the service frequent enough? Are buses used more heavily at certain times of the day?

The children may need to contact the local bus company, or conduct their own surveys, in order to obtain the necessary facts and figures.

Essential language
Timetable, arrive, depart, am, pm, hours, minutes, difference, compare, frequency, survey, tally, data.

ATs 1AB, 2DE, 9ABC, 12B, 13BCD.

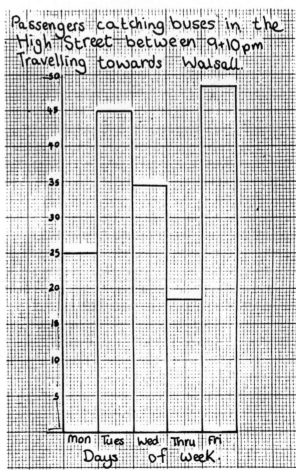

Passengers catching buses in the High Street between 9+10 pm Travelling towards Walsall.

Days of week.

Land use

The subject of land use can be brought into several topics. A look at land use locally raises environmental issues as well as developing aesthetic concern for the appearance of an area.

Begin by defining the area in which you are going to work, and select the appropriate Ordnance Survey maps. 1:1250 is the best scale to use, but this is available only for large towns and cities. If maps of this scale do not cover your area, use the most detailed map available.

Analysis

Look at the area covered by the map, and then classify it into a number of groups. Ask the children to think of possible groupings. They need to find categories for houses, services, industry etc.

Next, analyse the land use in the area and shade in the appropriate areas on the map. Do any areas remain unshaded? If so, can they be classified into one of the categories already used or do they need to be given a category of their own?

At this stage, look at the balance and proportion between the various categories. This can be done at a glance and an approximation made. It can then be analysed in greater depth as a basis for mathematical work on proportion, fractions and percentages. The information collected could be stored in a computer database developed by the children themselves.

Overlay

Each grid square on an Ordnance Survey map represents one square kilometre, or 1,000,000 square metres. This can be divided into 100 smaller squares which will be 100 metres × 100 metres or 10,000 square metres. Make an overlay of one square and then subdivide it into 100 squares.

Place the overlay on any of the grid squares and calculate the area taken up by each category (housing, services etc) by counting the squares. For example the children might count 25 squares for industrial use in one grid square.

This can then be expressed as a fraction

or percentage, $\dfrac{25 \text{ km}^2}{100} = 25$ per cent.

Work out the percentages for the other categories. What is the proportion of housing to open spaces for public use? What about the proportion of services to housing? How much waste land is there?

Calculate the total area of the map covered by each category and make comparisons between the areas covered by different categories.

Try investigating land use in a contrasting area; for example, compare a coastal area with a built-up area inland. Schools in contrasting areas could exchange information.

It would also be possible to include work on fractions and ratios related to decimals and percentages.

Variation

This activity can be linked with art. A pattern will emerge when the map is shaded according to the land usage. This pattern can be simplified and refined, enlarged or reduced until a pleasing design is found.

Then select a suitable medium to reproduce the design, for example paint, collage or embroidery.

Essential language

Square metre/kilometre/centimetre, overlay grid, more than, less than, half, estimate, irregular, approximate, row, multiply, length, breadth, width, subdivide, total area, compare, fraction, percentage, proportion, containing, equal.

ATs 1AB, 2DE, 8B, 9ABC, 12C.

Maths walks

Maths walks or maths trails have become very popular recently.

A number of schools have designed their own maths walk based on the school itself, both inside and out, or on the immediate area around the school. A maths walk can provide many cross-curricular links, as well as encouraging observation skills.

Outlined below are some of the types of activity you may wish to include.

Geography

The actual route that the walk follows could be considered; look at a large scale Ordnance Survey map, and investigate direction and location using coordinates or grid references. The children could practise using a compass to orientate themselves and locate landmarks.

Science and art

Look at structures and consider the ideas of shape, angle, symmetry, pattern, proportion and measurement.

Try to spot examples of the following architectural features:

- archways,
- doorways,
- brick bonding patterns,
- columns,
- the pitch of a roof,
- beams and girders.

Consider their construction, and use their design as a basis for artwork. Why are certain shapes normally associated with each of the architectural features?

English

Some aspects of Attainment Targets 1 and 3 in English can be developed by writing a commentary to fit in with a video or slide sequence of the trail.

Producing such a presentation can be a valuable experience, and the commentary could include much mathematical language.

Variation

Other aspects of mathematics can also be studied on a walk through a shopping area. Work can be carried out on subjects like time, money, price increases and decreases, percentages and VAT. There are plenty of interesting things to investigate. For example, a post office may display a timetable for the collection of mail, and have informative posters about the cost of sending letters to other countries. Shops display the prices of goods, and may sometimes pin up notices advertising a certain percentage off marked items. Banks display exchange rates which could be used to develop currency conversion graphs by children who have reached Level 5.

Essential language

Coordinates, grid references, scale, length, breadth, area, measurement, estimate, approximate, symmetry, angle, distance, direction, pattern, proportion, cost, price, percentage, money, increase, decrease, difference, exchange rate.

ATs 1AB, 2ADEF, 7, 8C, 9AB, 10AB, 11A, 12AC, 13B.

Minibeasts

Topic work involving the study of minibeasts provides an excellent context in which to develop children's skills in handling data, observation, classification and research.

Database

Discuss with the children which data concerning minibeasts they want to collect; perhaps the number of examples of each minibeast found in a certain location, or the number of minibeasts found which have no legs, six legs, eight legs or more than eight legs.

Collect the data using a frequency table and tallying methods and then represent the data using bar-line graphs.

Involve the children in the creation of a computer database to record the minibeasts they find. Discuss with them the headings (fields) which would be suitable for such a database. They might decide on something like the following:

Name: Woodlouse
Group: Arthropods
Family: Crustaceans
Length (mm): 18
Body parts: 2
Legs (pairs): 7
Wings (pairs): 0
Antennae: 4

Let the children interrogate the database they have created. Possible starting points are as follows:

- How many arachnids did you find?
- How many of the minibeasts have more than three pairs of legs?
- How many of the minibeasts have no wings?
- Which of the minibeasts have a length

less than 10mm?

The children can then present the sorted data in the form of bar-line graphs.

Commercially produced datafiles could also be used for the same sort of questioning and sorting.

Decision tree

A topic on minibeasts also provides an ideal situation for the development of identification keys, involving the children in the construction of decision tree diagrams. Here are some ideas for activities to help children formulate the sort of questions which will help them distinguish between different minibeasts.

Start by writing the names of five minibeasts on the board, and then play a game of 'twenty questions', where the children have to ask questions in order to discover the chosen minibeast. Tell the children that you can only answer 'yes' or 'no' to their questions. This activity provides the children with useful practice in asking the kind of questions necessary for building a successful decision tree diagram.

With the children working in small groups of four or five, present each group with a set of four or five minibeasts or pictures of minibeasts. Each child in turn removes one of the minibeasts, stating the characteristic which makes it different from the others.

This activity leads to the creation of decision trees. Discuss the children's reasons for removing each minibeast, and then ask them to write directions so that their friends can remove the same minibeast.

This can help the children develop simple keys. For example, using a set of minibeasts containing a slug, an ant, a centipede, a woodlouse and a butterfly, they could remove one minibeast at a time and write a question which distinguishes it from the others, as follows:
- Remove the slug.
  'Is it legless?
  If yes . . . it is a slug.
  If no . . . it might be an ant, centipede, woodlouse, or butterfly.'
- Remove the butterfly.
  'Does it have wings?

If yes . . . it is a butterfly.
  If no . . . it might be an ant, centipede or woodlouse.'
- Remove the ant.
  'Does it have six legs?
  If yes . . . it is an ant.
  If no . . . it might be a centipede or woodlouse.'
- Remove the centipede.
  'Does it have more than twelve pairs of legs?
  If yes . . . it is a centipede.
  If no . . . it is a woodlouse.'

The next stage is for the children to put in numbers to lead to subsequent questions:

This table can then be represented as a decision tree diagram as shown.

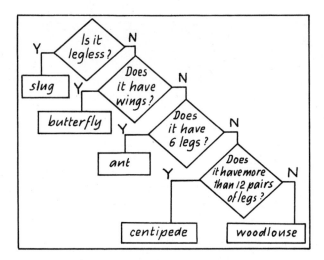

Extend this by asking the children to develop decision trees for larger sets of minibeasts in which the members of each set have less distinct differences. This demands a more critical observation and questioning technique.

For example, one group could be asked to create a decision tree diagram to help identify different species of spider.

Work of this nature can be enhanced by the use of computer programs specifically designed to develop children's ability to create decision tree diagrams.

Essential language

Frequency table, tally, bar-line graph, database, fields, interrogate, search, datafile, identification key, classify, decision tree diagram.

ATs 1AB, 2C, 8C, 9AB, 12AC, 13ABD.

114

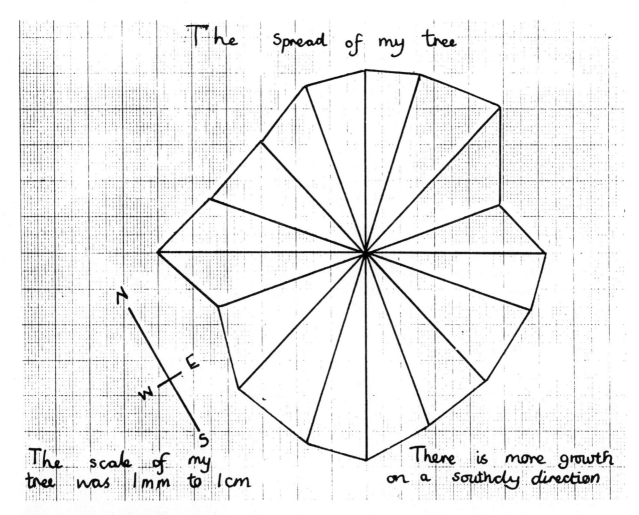

The spread of my tree

The scale of my tree was 1mm to 1cm

There is more growth on a southerly direction

The spread of a tree

The study of trees links in well with topics on plant life and on the wider environment. There is also considerable scope for mathematics when considering how to measure the spread of a tree or bush.

Using a suitable measuring instrument, measurements are taken which radiate from the foot of the tree to the furthest points reached by the overhanging branches. As well as giving practice in measuring, this activity can involve the use of the cardinal points of the compass.

When the measurements have been taken, the children can think of a way of recording them. Some children will appreciate the limitations of this method of measurement, and may suggest taking radiating measurements at smaller angular intervals.

If a scale diagram is drawn on squared paper and the ends of the measuring 'spokes' joined, the approximate area covered by the spread can be calculated by counting squares.

Results could be used to make comparisons between different species, localities and conditions.

Essential language

Angle, degree, metre, centimetre, millimetre.

ATs 1ABC, 8ABC, 9AB, 10A.

Testing materials

Science Attainment Target 6, which covers the types and uses of materials, provides an ideal context for some of the elements of the programme of study for mathematics at Level 4. Children are required to compare materials on the basis of properties such as strength, hardness, flexibility and solubility. They will have to devise experiments, and this will involve them in selecting the mathematics they will use in a task, and also in planning their work methodically and recording findings in an appropriate form.

Planning investigations

Science schemes and other books and periodicals offer many suggestions for activities testing building materials of different sorts. At Level 4, children are expected to 'raise questions in a form which can be investigated', and plan their own investigations. In doing this they will be using and extending their knowledge of measures.

Bricks

For instance, when testing the absorbency of bricks, children would have to decide how the amount of water the various bricks absorb could be measured. They would also have to take account of the variables involved. They may decide to measure the height to which the water rises, and perhaps also the speed of the rise. In this case the most appropriate measure would be millimetres, which will allow any small discrepancies to show up.

The children might decide to weigh the bricks dry and then again when they are saturated, and make comparisons on this basis. Or they might choose to test each brick individually and measure the final amount of water which has not been soaked up at the end of the experiment. In both these cases a small unit of measurement would offer the best scope for comparison.

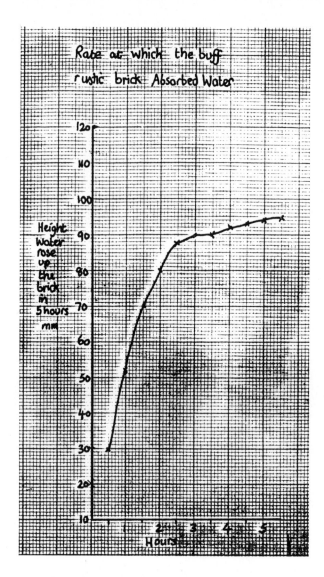

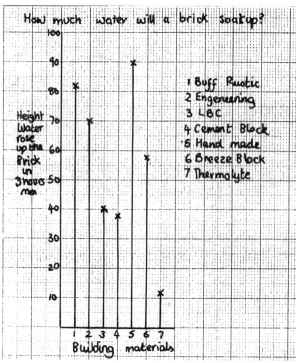

In making decisions of this sort, the children need to understand the relationship between different units; they also need to be able to make sensible estimates of a range of measures.

At this stage, children should also be selecting appropriate means of recording and presenting their results. In the above activity, for example, a line graph would be appropriate to show the rate at which an individual brick absorbs water. But if a child wanted to use one graph to show how much water each of the bricks absorbed, it would be better to use a bar chart or bar-line graph.

Essential language

Centimetre, millimetre, litre, millilitre, kilogram, gram, discrete data, axis, values, horizontal, vertical, line graph, bar-line graph, bar chart.

ATs 1AB, 8AC, 9AB, 12AB , 13BD.

Testing structures

Children learn through observation and experience to appreciate that some structures are stronger than others. At this level they will be able to make comparisons by using measures, recording results, and then presenting data by appropriate means.

Using given information, children will be able to construct their own three-dimensional shapes which can then be compared on the basis of their ability to withstand a force.

Further investigations could be conducted into the shapes; for example, try increasing the length or width of the faces of a triangular prism while keeping the other dimensions constant. The children could also test the effect of using bundles of shapes.

Essential language
Millimetre, centimetre, millilitre, litre, gram, kilogram, data, average, mean, bar-line graph, frequency, axis, horizontal, vertical.

ATs 1AB, 8AC, 9ABC, 12AB, 13BD.

Computer games

Computer games can provide good opportunities to combine enjoyment with some genuine and useful mathematical work at this level.

There are a number of programs on the market which use the theme of a quest; players have to locate a treasure or escape from a monster in order to win. Handled systematically games of this sort can give excellent experience in presenting and interpreting data and using mathematics to solve puzzles.

Many computer games involve moving through a maze or building. The children could make a systematic record of any information about the layout which comes to light, keeping careful notes of their explorations and drawing a plan. They could record the possible options and outcomes each time the game presents them with a variable in the form of a wizard, a monster, a magical object and so on.

Some programs actually include mathematical questions as part of the quest, but whether or not this is the case, there is still plenty of scope for mathematical thought.

Computer games provide good motivation for the children, and can also lead to a great amount of work away from the computer.

Essential language
Data, layout, plan, scale, variable.

ATs 1AB, 2A, 5B, 12A, 13A, 14AB.

Studying the past

Most areas of study involve the use of mathematics, and a look at the past is no exception. Children have natural interest in the lives and conditions of earlier generations which can be brought to life if they themselves are involved in making discoveries.

Resources
Census material provides a store of valuable material which can illuminate social conditions. Visit the local archivist to find appropriate material within the relevant dates, documenting particular areas and streets of interest.

117

Elmore Row. Blowich 1881

	Name	Head of family	Age	Rank, Profession or Occupation	Where born
1	Charles Walker	Head	34	Coal Miner	Rugalay
	Elizabeth Partridge		28	Housekeeper	Wordsley
2	Shadrack Ball	Head	30	Coal Miner	Bloxwich
	Sarah "	Wife	31	" " wife	
	Shadrack "	Son	4		"
3	John Walker	Head	40	Coal Miner	Rugeley
	Emma "	Wife	40	" " wife	Short Heath
	George E	Son	9	Scholar	Bloxwich
	John W.	Son	7	Scholar	"
	Benjamin	Son	4		"
	Hannah	Daughter	3		"
	Lucy	Daughter	5 months		"
	Charles Cox	Lodger	57	Coal Miner	not known
4	unoccupied				
5	George Broom	Head	58	Farm Labourer	Blimmel
	Eliza Broom	Wife	58	" " wife	Chattel
	Benjamin "	Son	19		Bloxwich
	Anne "	Daughter	12	Scholar	"
	Catherine "	Daughter	8	"	"

Once the information is acquired, enter it on to a disc or type it out, as the children may have difficulties with the original handwriting. You then have a marvellous resource which can only be fully interpreted with the application of mathematics.

Gather information on the following areas:
- The average number of children in families.
- The average size of a household.
- The range of occupations in which people were involved.
- The most popular names.

Registers of baptisms and deaths from local parish churches also provide opportunities to use mathematics to understand more about the past.

Essential language
Average, mean.

ATs 1ABC, 9AB.

Number systems

Children are fascinated by other number systems, and studying one from the ancient world will give impetus to a study of former civilisations. Children will be able to examine other cultures, while considering place values and the economy of our own number system.

Here are some number systems which give opportunities for historical and geographical study in addition to mathematical activity.

- Sumerians wrote numbers on clay tablets with a pointed stick, which formed the wedge-shaped symbols known as cuneiform (in Latin, *cuneus* means 'wedge'). The tablets were baked in the sun or in a fire.

$$(1 \times 600) + (2 \times 60) + (5 \times 10) + (7 \times 1) = 777$$

Use this idea to inspire designs for clay tiles.

The Sumerians understood the notion of place value, using the same symbols in different positions to represent different numbers.

• In hieroglyphics the Egyptian number system looked like this.

The number 3786 could be represented in extended notation as shown.

1	2	3	4	5	6

|||| |||	|||| ||||	||| ||| |||	∩	9	⌒	⌐
7	8	9	10	100	1000	10000

$$(3 \times 1000) + (7 \times 100) + (8 \times 10) + (6 \times 1)$$

• The numerals presently in use in China have been in use since ancient times.

Place value is indicated by vertical rather than horizontal alignment.

~	≈	≋	⟡	玉
1	2	3	4	5

六	七	八	允	十	百
6	7	8	9	10	100

十 六	六 十	玉 十 六	六 玉
16	60	106	600

• Hindu notation around 800 AD was the first to use a symbol as a place filler – an idea which we have subsequently found very valuable.

Essential language
Position, column, digit, symbol, thousand, hundred, ten, unit, grouping.

ATs 2ABF, 3AB, 5AB.

Turtle geometry

At this level the experience of using LOGO commands to move a floor turtle can be used to develop children's ability to specify location by means of angle and distance.

To get the turtle to turn through a certain angle, LOGO uses the complement of the angle (otherwise known as the exterior angle).

In order to draw an angle whose interior angle is 60 degrees, the turtle would therefore have to turn 120 degrees to the right.

Once the children are familiar with the commands and can visualise approximately the distance the turtle will cover when they type in various commands, the possibilities are endless. Using LOGO the children can draw a whole variety of two-dimensional shapes; perhaps a car, a house, a lunar landscape, spirals, insects, a plan of house, and many other things besides.

Essential language
Angle, turn, distance, direction, LOGO, commands, forwards, backwards, right, left, repeat, procedure.

ATs 1C, 9C, 10AB, 11A.

Fenced in

Given that a rectangle has a perimeter of 28 centimetres, can the children find its length and width so that it covers the largest possible area?

Let them use their own ways of tackling the problem, perhaps trying different methods and improving on them.

Once they have discovered the solution to the problem, which is a seven centimetre square of area 49 square centimetres, they may plot all their different results on a graph. They will need to order the rectangles according to the size of their areas.

The graph produces a parabolic curve. Ask the children to explain the graph to you in their own words. What can they tell you about it?

Variation

Finding the largest possible area for rectangles with perimeters which are multiples of four will result in squaring numbers. For example, if the perimeter is 24 centimetres, then the answer will be a square with sides of six centimetres, producing an area of 36 square centimetres.

Try experimenting with perimeters which are not multiples of four. What conclusions can the children draw now?

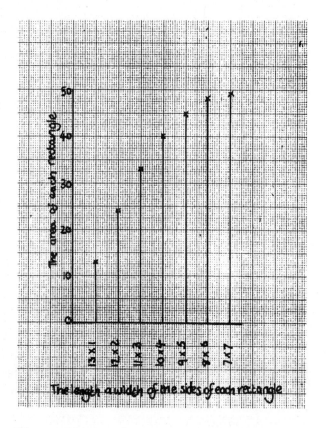

The results may be graphed in the same way, and the graphs compared. What do the children notice?

Essential language

Rectangle, measure, length, width, area, perimeter, centimetre, square centimetre, square numbers, graph.

ATs 1AB, 8B, 10B, 13C.

How many squares?

How many squares can the children see on this grid?

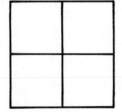

This investigation invites the children to discover the following relationship: to calculate the total number of possible squares in a grid, square the number of units in a side of the grid, and square any numbers less than the number of units in a side. The total number of squares in a grid is the total of these answers.

What you need
Squared paper, graph paper, rulers.

What to do
This activity can be explored by looking at grids of sizes from 1×1 to 8×8 (chessboard size) and beyond.

A systematic approach to this problem is required.

First start with a grid of only one square. Record the number of squares you can find.

Then count the number of squares on a 2 × 2 grid. Record:
- the number of small squares,
- the number of large squares,
- the total number of squares.

Next, count the number of squares on a 3 × 3 grid. Record:
- the number of small squares,

121

- the number of corner (2 × 2) squares,
- the number of large (3 × 3) squares,
- the total number of squares.

Continue the investigation with grids of other sizes. As the grids get bigger there will be possible squares in the middle as well as at the corners; don't forget to count all the possibilities.

If possible, encourage the children to devise their own ways of recording and solving the problem. Allow them the opportunity to discover for themselves the pattern which involves squaring numbers.

The results may be graphed in the following way:

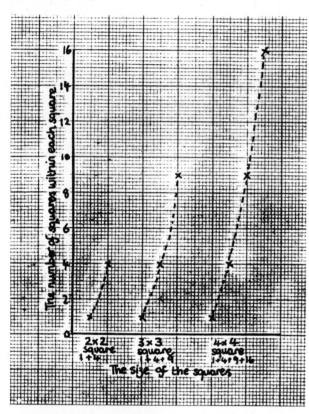

Essential language
Add, plus, total, multiply, grid, times, square numbers, patterns, predict.

ATs 1ABC, 5B, 6A, 13C.

Diagonals

This is an investigation into the number of squares in a rectangular grid that are crossed by the diagonal of the rectangle. The children have to look for a relationship between the length and breadth of the rectangle and the number of squares crossed by its diagonal.

122

This relationship may be expressed as L + B − HCF, where HCF is the highest common factor of the length and breadth.

What you need
Squared paper, graph paper, rulers.

What to do
Ask the children to draw and experiment with lots of different rectangles, and to keep a tabulated record of their findings.

As the children develop their table of results, ask them whether they can see any kind of relationship between the length and breadth of each rectangle and the number of squares crossed by its diagonal.

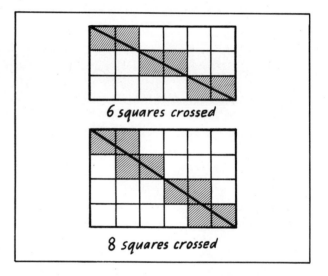

6 squares crossed

8 squares crossed

At first the children may suggest that the relationship is L + B − 1, as the majority of their examples will produce such a relationship. In this case, point out examples which do not fit this generalisation, but at the same time encourage them by suggesting that they are close to finding the relationship.

length	breadth	squares crossed by diagonal
6	3	6
6	4	8

Graphing the results obtained from rectangles of a specific length with varying breadths may help in revealing the relationship. A line graph such as the one which follows clearly shows the emergence of a pattern.

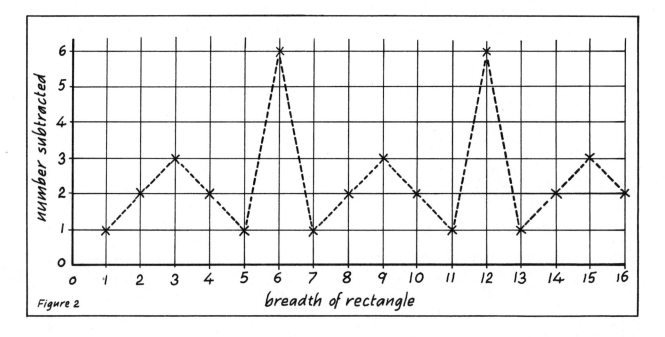

Figure 2

At this level, the children should only be expected to express the relationship in words. For example, 'To find the number of squares that are crossed by the diagonal of a rectangle, you add together the length and the breadth then take away the highest number that will divide equally into both the length and the breadth.'

After they have discovered the relationship, ask the children to test their statements by applying them to specific examples, and checking this by drawing.

Essential language

Square, rectangle, grid, diagonal, relationship, findings, results, table, tabulate, divide, add, subtract, generalisation, solution, pattern, line graph.

ATs 1ABC, 5AB, 6A, 13C.

Bounce

'Bounce' is an investigation involving the rebounds made by an imaginary ball on snooker-type tables of varying sizes.

What you need

Squared paper, graph paper, rulers.

What to do

Imagine rolling a ball at 45 degrees from the top left-hand corner of a rectangular grid. When the ball meets a side of the grid it rebounds inwards at an angle of 90 degrees, and finally stops when it reaches a corner.

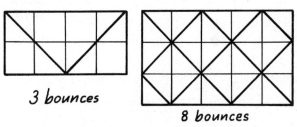

3 bounces

8 bounces

Ask the children whether they can discover the number of bounces the ball will make as it travels round rectangles of different sizes. The total number of bounces includes the starting and finishing corners.

Ask the children to keep a record of their results in the form of a table.

Ask the children to look carefully at their table of results, and see if they can suggest a relationship between the length and breadth of the rectangle and the number of bounces made by the ball.

The relationship that the children are trying to discover is that the total number of bounces is equal to the length of the rectangle plus the breadth, divided by the highest common factor of the length and the breadth.

If used with a large group, the investigation would provide a good opportunity for sharing tasks, combining results and working co-operatively. Ask the children to develop a way of dividing up the task so that many different examples are tried and none are duplicated.

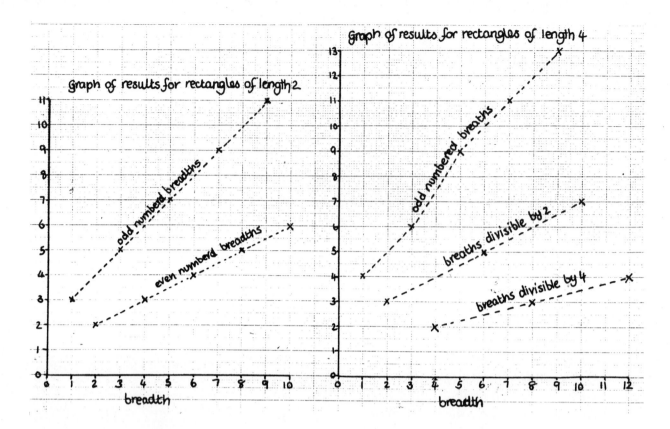

Graph of results for rectangles of length 2

Graph of results for rectangles of length 4

As an aid to the discovery of the relationship, line graphs such as the one shown could be developed for rectangles with a constant length, but having varying breadths.

The graph showing the results for rectangles two units in length shows two trends, one for the odd-numbered breadths and another for the even-numbered breadths. Discuss these trends with the children in order to discover a relationship.

Graphs for rectangles of other lengths will reveal different trends. They can all be used in discussion to help the children to discover the relationship. For example, the graph for the results of rectangles four units in length reveals three trends; one for odd-numbered breadths, one for breadths divisible by two and one for breadths divisible by four.

Discuss with the children both the tabulated results and the graphs, in order to tease out the relationship.

At this level, children would only be expected to express the relationship in words, for example: 'To find the number of bounces, first add the length and the breadth then divide by the highest number that will divide equally into both the length and the breadth.'

124

Essential language
Right angle, angle, degrees, rectangular, grid, rebound, length, breadth, relationship, highest common factor, line graph, trend, results, table, tabulate, divide, add.

ATs 1ABC, 5B, 6A, 10A, 13C.

Throwing a die

This is an activity to extend children's knowledge of probability and to provide opportunities for graph work arising from real experiences.

What you need
For each pair of children, a six-sided die and some graph paper.

What to do
Ask the children to look closely at their die.
• How many faces has it?
• What numbers are shown on each face?
• What is the sum of the numbers on opposite faces?
Ask the children about the probability of throwing certain scores on the die.
• If the die is thrown once, what scores can we get?

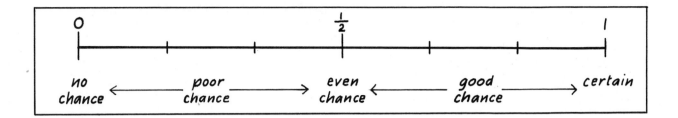

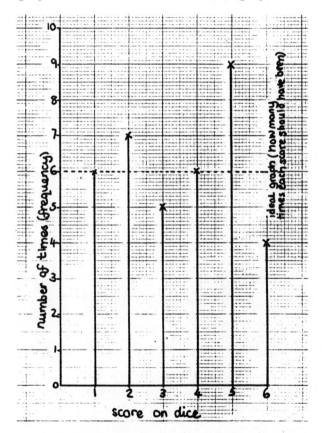

- If the die is thrown six times, how many times can we expect to score 6?
- If the die is thrown six times, how many times can we expect to score an odd number?
- If the die is thrown once, what is the chance of scoring a 6?
- If the die is thrown once, what is the chance of scoring an odd number?
- If the die is thrown once, what is the chance of scoring a 5 or 6?

Relate the last three questions to the probability scale from 0 to 1.

As there are six possible outcomes when throwing a die, the chance (probability) of throwing each of the scores is as follows:
- The probability of throwing a 6 with one throw is one in six, recorded as a probability of 1/6.
- The probability of throwing an odd number with one throw is three in six (evens), or 3/6.
- The probability of throwing a 5 or 6 with one throw is two in six, or 2/6.

Discuss Cardan's formula for calculating probability. This involves dividing the number of favourable outcomes by the total number of possible outcomes.

This can be related back to the probability scale from 0 to 1, divided into sixths as we are dealing with six possible outcomes.

Ask the children to predict the number of times they would score 6 if they were to throw the die 36 times. Test their predictions, working in pairs with one partner throwing the die while the other tallies the result of each throw.

Next, ask the children to display their results in a bar-line graph, first graphing the ideal results using a dotted line.

Compare the results with the predictions. What do the children notice?

Ask each pair of children to compare the graph of their own results with those of other pairs. What do they notice?

Combine the results on a table, as below.

Display this information in a bar-line graph or a frequency diagram, first graphing the ideal results using a dotted line.

Discuss the differences between the graph of combined results and the graphs of the results of each pair. The children should notice that the results shown on the combined graph are much closer to the 'ideal graph'. Point out to the children that the more trials made in a probability experiment, the more likely it is that the results will be close to the 'ideal' results.

score	A	B	C	D	E	F	total
1	6	4	7	5	8	6	36
2	7	8	5	6	4	5	35

Variations

Using two coins:
- What are the possible outcomes of throwing both coins once?
- What is the probability of throwing two heads?

Using a pack of playing cards:
- What is the probability of drawing certain groups of cards, such as a court card, an ace or a club?

Let the children devise their own experiments involving drawing coloured cubes or beads from a bag.

Essential language

Die, dice, faces, odd, even, chance, probability, probability scale, possible outcomes, evens, favourable cases, tally chart, bar-line graph, ideal graph, frequency diagram, predict.

ATs 2D, 9BC, 12AB, 13D, 14ABC.

All aboard

This is an example of a mathematical problem which may be solved by the use of a particular strategy, that of tabulating, identifying and continuing a pattern.

What you need

Graph paper, pencils.

What to do

Consider this situation:

'An empty train picked up two passengers at the first stop. At every stop thereafter, it picked up three more passengers than at the previous stop. How many passengers got on at the tenth stop? How many passengers altogether were on the train when it left the tenth stop?'

The first stage in solving the problem is to read and understand the problem:

Ask the children:
- What do we know for certain?
- What are we trying to find out?

Once the problem statement is understood, the next stage is to plan a solution.

Discuss ways of representing the information given in the problem statement. Consider how this could be

126

extended in order to develop the pattern and solve the problem. This should lead to some form of tabulated recording:

stop	1	2	3	4	5	6	7	8	9	10
passengers getting on	2	5	8	11	14	17	20	23	26	29
total passengers	2	7	15	26	40	57	77	100	126	155

The problem is solved by continuing the pattern in the table. By referring to the table it can be seen that 29 passengers boarded the train at the tenth stop and that a total of 155 passengers were on the train when it left the tenth stop.

Although it now seems that the required solution has been found, there is still one more important stage of the problem solving process to be gone through, that of looking back to the problem statement and checking the answer.

Ask the children:
- Have you used all the important data?
- Are your calculations correct?
- Does the answer make sense?
- Does the answer fit the problem?

One way of checking whether the pattern has been developed successfully is to construct a line graph:

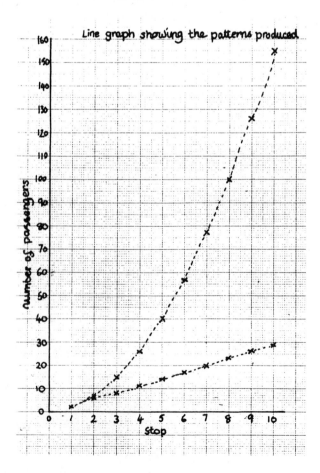

Line graph showing the patterns produced

The lines on the graph representing each of the two patterns in the problem show a regular growth, indicating that each of the patterns has been developed correctly.

'All aboard' is only one example of a problem which involves the recognition and development of patterns. It is quite easy to invent others to give the children experience with different number patterns.

Essential language
Table, tabulate, pattern, solution, solve, problem, data, calculations, line graph.

ATs 1BC, 3B, 5AB, 6A.

Hexagons

This activity develops the ability to recognise and design shapes which have rotational symmetry.

What you need
Coloured paper, rulers, scissors, adhesive, sticky tape, paper-fasteners.

What to do
Start by cutting out four congruent equilateral triangles with a side of 12cm. The triangles can be cut from two contrasting colours. Then fold the triangles along one axis of symmetry and cut on that line. You will now only need three triangles of each colour.

Arrange the triangles like this. You have constructed a pattern with rotational symmetry of order six.

The triangles can now be stuck down into position, or the activity can be extended. Try changing the shape of the triangles by snipping into the outer angle of each one (make sure the cuts are identical) to form a design such as this.

The children could make other similar patterns, and then the finished patterns can be made to rotate by placing them on to larger pieces of paper and securing in the centre with a paper-fastener.

Variation
Use eight triangles for the design, starting the activity with four congruent squares which can be cut along the diagonal. What order of rotational symmetry would this design have?

Essential language
Congruent, equilateral triangles, measure, axis of line symmetry, rotational symmetry, angle, 60 degree angle.

ATs 11B.

Constructing houses

This activity can tie in well with various topics. To link in with a local history project or work on the local environment children might construct models of buildings of local interest, or of their own houses. Making houses can also form part of a topic on buildings or housing in the wider sense. The task of model-making involves knowledge and understanding of

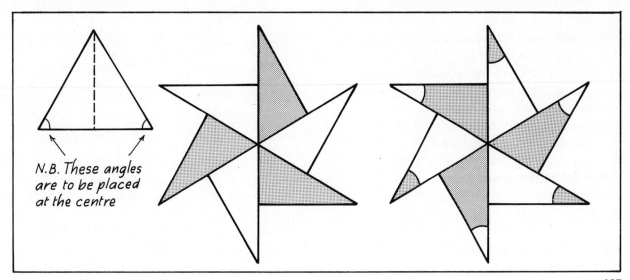

N.B. These angles are to be placed at the centre

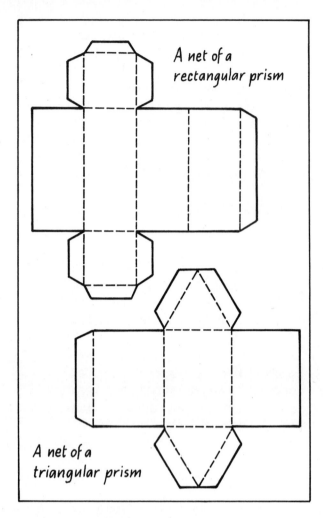

A net of a rectangular prism

A net of a triangular prism

the properties of two- and three-dimensional shapes.

What you need
Thin card, rulers, scissors, sticky tape, adhesive, pens, paints.

What to do
Let the children make nets for cubes and rectangular and triangular prisms which can be assembled to make buildings. The children can decorate these, and cut out pieces to create windows and doors.

If larger rectangular prisms are constructed, one of the faces can be cut away to leave an open box or room which can be decorated and furnished. Make a large model house by fixing a number of such rectangular prisms together.

Essential language
Cube, cuboid, rectangular prism, triangular prism, pyramid, triangle, rectangle, circle, net.

ATs 1A, 8A, 9A, 10B.

128

Religious symbols

Many religious symbols lend themselves to work involving angles, symmetry and the construction of two-dimensional shapes.

The Star of David
This activity explores a number of ways of making a Star of David.

What you need
Paper, compasses, scissors, ruler, isometric paper.

What to do
• Draw a circle with a radius of six centimetres. Use a pair of compasses set at six centimetres to mark off points round the circle at a six-centimetre interval. Join alternate points with a straight line to make a Star of David.
• Draw a 12-point 'clock', and mark and join the multiples of four to form both intersecting triangles.
• To make a folded paper Star of David, first draw and cut out a circle. Mark its centre, and fold the circle so that the circumference touches the centre.

Fold a second time from one of the corners of the first fold, so that once again the circumference touches the centre.

Now fold a third time in the same way in order to form an equilateral triangle.

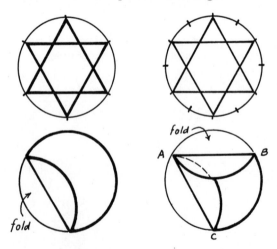

Now fold point A to the centre, then similarly with points B and C, thus forming a second equilateral triangle.

Rule lines along each of the folds to reveal the Star of David.

Other activities with the Star of David

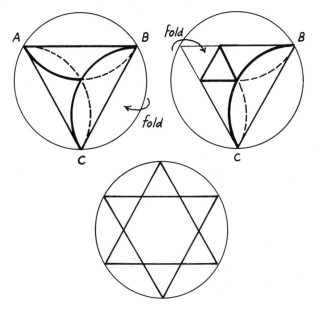

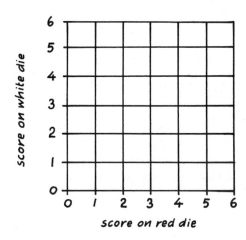

include:
- Investigating the axes of line symmetry.
- Investigating the size of angles.
- Drawing the symbol in different sizes on isometric paper and investing the number of triangles it encloses as the symbol increases in size.

Carry out similar investigations into the shape and symmetry of other religious symbols:

Christianity – the cross
Islam – the crescent and the star
Buddhism – the wheel

Essential language
Circle, circumference, radius, triangle, hexagon, angle, line symmetry.

ATs 2DE, 3BC, 4ABC, 10AB, 11B.

Four-by-four

This is a game for two players involving locating points by means of coordinates.

What you need
For each pair of children, a game board and a pair of dice of different colours, numbered one to six.

What to do
Each player has a symbol (either a nought or a cross), and each aims to arrange their symbols in a winning arrangement; that is, in a vertical, horizontal or diagonal row of four, or in the form of a 2 × 2 square.

The board is simply a 6 × 6 grid of squares, with each axis numbered from zero to six as shown. Each axis corresponds to one of the dice.

Players take turns in rolling the two dice.

The scores on each die indicate the position at which the players place their symbols. For example, Player A throws one on the red die and four on the white die, and plots an X at position (1, 4) on the grid, as shown.

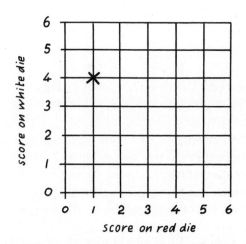

The game continues with each player throwing the dice in turn and plotting the resulting ordered pair on the grid until one player succeeds in creating a winning arrangement of their symbols.

If a player lands on a position already occupied by a symbol, he or she misses that turn.

Variations
Many other games using the same equipment and the same basic rules as 'Four-by-four' are possible. Try changing

the requirements for winning the game, so players win by joining adjacent points to create a 'bridge' between two opposite sides of the board, or compete to capture the points which make up the last side of a square.

Essential language
Coordinates, ordered pair, address, row, column, grid, axis, horizontal, vertical, diagonal.

ATs 7, 11A.

Along the dragon's back

This is a calculator game for two players. It introduces and develops the idea of the inverse relationship of multiplication and division and provides practise with multiplication facts up to 10×10.

What you need
For each pair of players, two copies of the board, each with different numbers (see photocopiable page 185); two counters; a calculator.

What to do
The aim is to be first to reach the last number on the dragon's back, using multiplication and division to move along the scales.

To begin the game, each player places their counter on the first number on the left of their 'dragon's back' board.

In turn the players enter their first number into the calculator and attempt to change it to the number on the top of the first scale by using only multiplication or division.

A successful attempt allows the player to move their counter up to the top of the first scale. Unsuccessful attempts require the player to wait and try again at the next turn.

After reaching the top of the first scale, the player then has to move to the base of the next scale in the same way as before. This will mean performing an operation which is the inverse of the one before; if moving to the first tip meant multiplying two by four to make eight, moving down to

the next base will mean dividing eight by four to make two again.

The players continue in this way until one of them reaches the last number on their dragon's back and wins the game.

Essential language
Multiply, multiplied by, divide, divided by, factor, product, dividend, divisor, quotient, inverse.

ATs 3A, 6B.

Beat the goalie

This game for two players will require children to read a calculator display to the nearest whole number.

What you need
For each pair of children, a number line and 'goalie' as shown, and a calculator.

What to do
The first stage is to draw a number line which contains ten to twelve points. Any two of these numbers are then selected as points at which to place the uprights of the goalposts.

Each player is then allowed five shots at goal. The player not shooting at the time, the 'defender', places the goalkeeper card on the line and offers a number to the player who is shooting; for example, the number 53.

In order to score a goal, the 'attacking' player must find another number to divide this number by in order to produce an answer which will hit the number line between the uprights, while at the same time avoiding the numbers covered by the goalkeeper. For example, 53 divided by three is 17.66666667.

The shot is then marked by placing a cross on the number line. Goals are only allowed if the cross is placed quite accurately on the number line.

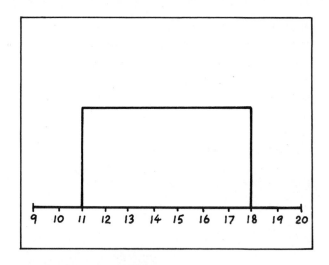

Essential language
Multiply, divide, approximate, approximately, round up, round down, display.

ATs 3A, 4BC.

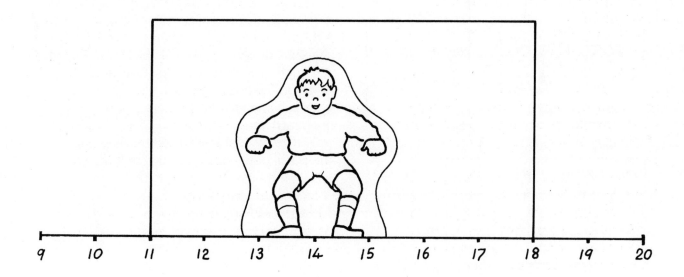

Polyominoes

This is a dice game for two players, involving knowledge of area and rotational symmetry.

What you need
For each two players, a copy of the board, a pair of dice numbered one to six, and coloured pencils or pens.

What to do
Make a board consisting of a 10cm × 10cm grid of squares. The playing shapes are eleven different 'polyominoes' (different arrangements of squares which are joined by common edges), as shown.

The aim of the game is to win the most polyominoes, and cover the largest amount of the board.

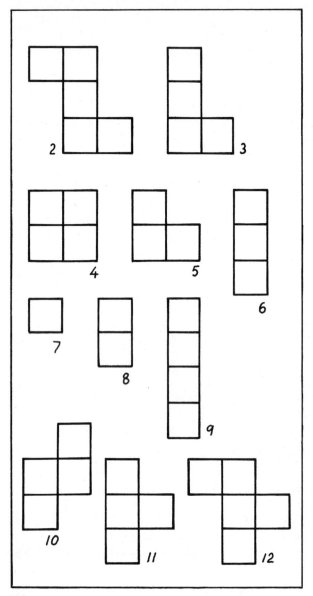

Give the children a picture of the different polyominoes to remind them during the game. The number indicated under each polyomino represents the score needed to win it.

Players take turns to roll both dice and add the scores. The total indicates the shape to be drawn on the board.

The relevant shape is then drawn anywhere on the board and is coloured using the player's colour. When drawing the shape, the player may orientate it in any way, perhaps reflecting or rotating it. Play continues in this way until one player is unable to draw his or her shape on the board, at which point the game ends.

At the end of the game each player finds the total area of the board that is occupied by his or her shapes, the winner being the player whose shapes occupy the greater area.

Ask the children to consider the following questions in relation to the game:
● What is the area of each shape?
● What is the area of the board?
● In how many different ways can each shape be drawn?
● Which of the shapes is the easiest to place on the board and why?
● Which shape is the hardest to place on the board and why?

The game could be varied by changing the set of polyominoes or by changing the size of the board.

Essential language
Area, square, dice, reflect, rotate, total area, square centimetres, cm^2.

ATs 8B, 11AB.

Badminton

'Badminton' is a calculator game for two players which involves the mental addition and subtraction of two-digit numbers by counting on or back, and using estimation and approximation to check the calculations (Attainment Targets 3 and 4).

What you need
For each pair of children, a calculator, one coloured die to represent tens, one coloured die to represent units, and two scoresheets.

What to do
Each player aims to score 11 points and win the game.

To begin, Player A 'serves' a two-digit number to Player B by entering it into the calculator; for example, Player A might enter 64.

Player B makes a note of this number in the 'number in display' column of the scoresheet, and then rolls both dice and makes a note of the resulting number in the 'target' column; for example, Player B rolls a four and a two and writes down 42.

Player B then has to change the number in the calculator display into the 'target number' by either addition or subtraction,

first estimating the result. In this case, Player B would perform the following mental calculations:

- $64 - ? = 42$
- Estimate: $60 - 20 = 40$
- Counting back: $64 - 4 = 60$; $60 - 10 = 50$; $50 - 8 = 42$
- Therefore: $64 - \mathbf{22} = 42$

Player B then enters 'minus 22' into the calculator, to leave the display reading 42, the required target.

If Player B is successful, the calculator is passed to Player A, leaving the current number in the display (42 in this case).

Player A now rolls both dice and then proceeds as above in order to change the number currently in the display into the new 'target number' generated by rolling the dice.

Play continues in this way until one player makes an error, which gives one point to the other player.

The player winning the point then 'serves' another two-digit number to the other player.

Essential language
Tens, units, add, subtract, count on, count back, difference, estimate, total, sum.

ATs 3B, 4A.

player	number in display	'target' number	estimate	key presses	display	points A	points B
B	*64	42	$60 - \underline{20} = 40$	☐ 22 ☐	42		
A	42	15	$40 - \underline{20} = 20$	☐ 27 ☐	15		
B	15	37	$20 + \underline{20} = 40$	☐ 22 ☐	37		
A	37	66	$40 + \underline{30} = 70$	☐ 26 ☐	63		1
A	*78	24	$80 - \underline{60} = 20$	☐ 54 ☐	24		
B	24	52	$20 + \underline{30} = 50$	☐ 28 ☐	52		
A	52	13	$50 - \underline{40} = 10$	☐ 38 ☐	14		2

☀ indicates the number 'served'

Level 4 glossary of terms

The following glossary explains some of the mathematical terms which are contained within the statements of attainment for mathematics at Level 4.

Acute angle
An angle less than 90 degrees.

Class intervals
Groups into which data is collected; for example, data concerning children's scores in a test, with marks out of fifty, could be collected in the following groups: 0–9, 10–19, 20–29, 30–39, 40–50. Such data is referred to as grouped data.

Coordinates
Ordered pairs of numbers which describe the position of a point in relation to two axes. The first number in the pair refers to the position of the point in relation to the horizontal axis (x-axis), and the second refers to the vertical axis (y-axis). In the diagram, the coordinates of the point marked are (2, 4).

Coordinates in the first quadrant
Coordinates in which both numbers of the ordered pair are positive, the first quadrant being the area above the x-axis and to the right of the y-axis.

Discrete data
Information concerning discrete variables, ie those which are separate from one another, such as colour of eyes, days, scores or shoe sizes.

Equations
Mathematical sentences or number sentences which assert that two values are equal; for example 3+7=6+4 or 8+4=12.

Equivalence
The property of having the same value, as with this equivalent class of fractions:
$$\frac{1}{2} \quad \frac{2}{4} \quad \frac{3}{6} \quad \frac{4}{8} \quad \frac{5}{20} \quad \frac{6}{12}$$

Frequency table
A table which shows how often an event or quantity occurs.

Generalise a pattern
To represent the common characteristics of a pattern with a general statement which applies equally to each individual element in the pattern.

Horizontal
Exactly level, parallel to the horizon.

Inverse operations
Arithmetic operations that are opposites. Addition is the inverse of subtraction, and multiplication is the inverse of division.

Multiplication facts
Another term for multiplication tables.

Nearest whole number
Reading a calculator display of, say 45.6022, to the nearest whole number would involve a process of rounding up or rounding down, according to the digit in the tenths position. In this case the display would be read as 46 to the nearest whole number (rounded up as the .6 is greater than .5).

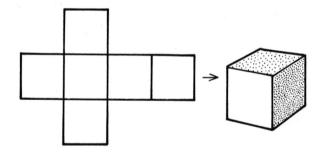

Net
A plane (two-dimensional) shape that when folded will form a solid (three-dimensional) shape.

Obtuse angle
An angle greater than 90 degrees, but less than 180 degrees.

Parallel
Parallel lines are an equal distance apart along their whole length.

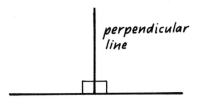

perpendicular line

Perpendicular
At right angles to the horizontal.

Probability
The chance or likelihood of an event happening.

Reflex angle
An angle greater than 180 degrees.

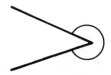

Relationship between units
Understanding of the relationship between units involves knowing, for example, that:
1000mm=1m
1mm=0.001m
100cm=1m
1cm=0.01m

Rotational symmetry
A shape is said to have rotational symmetry if after a rotation of less than 360 degrees it forms an identical image of itself.

A triangle has rotational symmetry of order 3

Rounding errors
According to their operating systems different calculators either round off or truncate recurring decimals, as the following examples show:
- 2÷3=0.666666 – this calculator truncates.
- 2÷3=0.666667 – this calculator rounds off.

These different systems have an effect on operations such as 2÷3×3. Children need to be aware of this reason for calculators producing an answer such as 1.9999999 for this operation.

Simple formulae
Equations which use symbols to represent simple relationships between quantities; eg the simple formula for the volume of a cuboid:
$v = l \times b \times h$ where 'v' = volume, 'l' = length, 'b' = breadth, 'h' = height.

Simple fractions
Also known as common fractions, vulgar fractions or rational numbers. Ordinary fractions where both the numerator and denominator are whole numbers (integers).

Statement
A definition of a mathematical pattern or relationship.

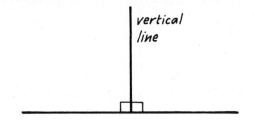

Tallying
A way of recording data as it is collected, using single 'stick' marks which are grouped into fives.

Vertical
Exactly upright; at right angles to the horizontal.

vertical line

Level 4: Programme of Study

This diagram shows how the programme of study can be expanded, suggesting teaching stages where applicable.

- Represent numbers to 10000 using Multibase, abacuses and extended notation.
- Use < and > to order pairs of numbers.
- Arrange numbers in ascending and descending orders.
- Represent numbers verbally and numerically.
- Understand the value of each digit.

- Represent numbers to 10000 by listing the numbers of units, tens, hundreds and thousands they contain.

- Make fractions by folding and cutting, shading, dividing shapes on a pinboard.
- Shade a unit fraction of a given shape.
- Understand fractional notation.
- Shade non-unit fractions of a given shape.
- Find fractions of quantities.

- Learn multiplication facts in different ways.
- Use multiplication facts in everyday situations.

- Use the 'spotting tens' strategy – eg:
$$6 + 3 + 9 + 4 + 7 =$$
$$10 + 10 + 9 = 29$$

- Understand the distributive law, eg $29 \times 3 = (20 \times 3) + (9 \times 3)$.
- Multiply multiples of ten by a single digit.
- Multiply two-digit numbers by a single digit, using extended, then conventional notation.
- Identify factors of equations whose two-digit answers are not exact products, eg. $[ ] \times 7 < 51$.
- Use 'box notation' for remainders, within tables.
- Divide two-digit numbers by a single digit using extended notation.
- Divide a two-digit number by a single digit using conventional notation.
- Divide a two-digit number by a single digit using Multibase and decomposition, to lead to conventional notation.

Using and applying mathematics
- Select the materials and the mathematics to use for a task and plan work methodically.
- Record findings and present them in oral, written or visual form.
- Use examples to test statements or definitions.

Number
- Read, write and order whole numbers.
- Understand and use the effect of multiplying whole numbers by 10 or 100.
- Use, with understanding, decimal notation to two decimal places in the context of measurement.
- Understand and use the relationship between place values in whole numbers.
- Recognise and understand simple fractions.
- Recognise and understand simple percentages.
- Know multiplication facts up to 10×10 and use them in multiplication and division problems.
- Add and subtract mentally two two-digit numbers.
- Add mentally single-digit numbers.
- Add and subtract two three-digit numbers, without a calculator.
- Multiply and divide two-digit numbers by a single-digit number, without a calculator.
- Estimate and approximate to check the validity of addition and subtraction calculations.
- Read calculator displays to the nearest whole number and know how to interpret results which have rounding errors.
- Solve addition and subtraction problems using numbers with no more than two decimal places, and multiplication and division problems starting with whole numbers.

- Multiply by ten and multiples of ten, noting digit shift.
- Multiply by 100 and multiples of 100, noting digit shift.
- Apply digit shift to mental calculations.

- Record measurements on a decimal abacus.
- Record measurements in column form.
- Record measurements in decimal form, where the decimal point separates the whole units from the parts of a unit.

- Understand that 'percentage' means 'out of 100'.
- Shade given percentages of a 100 square.

- Add two-digit numbers mentally, using rounding up and rounding down strategies.
- Subtract two-digit numbers mentally by
a) equal addition:
$$83 \rightarrow + 3 \rightarrow = 86$$
$$-\underline{27} \rightarrow + 3 \rightarrow = \underline{30}$$
$$56$$
b) counting on:
$$83 - 27$$
$$27 + 3 = 30 + 50 = 80 + 3 = 83, \text{ so}$$
$$27 + 56 = 83.$$

- Use extended notation, no exchange.
- Use conventional notation, no exchange.
- Use extended notation with exchange, first in one column and then in two.
- Use conventional notation with exchange, first in one column and then in two.

- Check by rounding up or down to the nearest ten.

Level 4: Programme of Study (continued)

- Find the weight, length and capacity of objects greater than one kilogram, metre or litre, and read to the nearest division of the measuring instrument used.
- Use a range of different measuring equipment.
- Understand the quantities represented by the divisions between numbers on a scale.
- Record in the appropriate metric measure, including the use of decimal notation.

Algebra
- Explore properties of numbers including equivalence of fractions.
- Generalise patterns, *eg symmetry of results*.
- Understand and use simple formulae or equations expressed in words.
- Recognise that multiplication and division are inverse operations and use this to check calculations.
- Know the conventions of the coordinate representation of points; work with coordinates in the first quadrant.

Measures
- Understand the relationship between units.
- Find areas by counting squares, and volumes by counting cubes.
- Make sensible estimates of a range of measures in relation to everyday objects.

Shape and space
- Understand and use language associated with angle.
- Construct two-dimensional and three-dimensional shapes from given information.
- Specify location by means of coordinates in the first quadrant and by means of angle and distance.
- Recognise rotational symmetry.

Handling data
- Specify an issue for which data are needed.
- Collect and group discrete data, using frequency tables and block graphs with suitable equal class intervals.
- Understand, calculate and use the mean and range of a set of data.
- Interrogate data in a computer database.
- Construct and interpret bar-line and line graphs and frequency diagrams with suitable class intervals for discrete variables.
- Create a decision-tree diagram.
- Understand and use probability scale from 0 to 1.
- Give and justify subjective estimates of probabilities.
- List all the possible outcomes of an event.

- Introduce the concept of volume as a measure of 'space taken'.
- Fill a box with cubes, leaving no space.
- Build regular shapes using centimetre cubes, and record dimensions by counting cubes.
- Build different cuboids using the same number of cubes – conservation of volume.
- Build sets of centimetre cubes into shapes of given dimensions.

- Recognise the need for a standard unit to measure area.
- Find the areas of rectangles by counting squares.
- Make different rectangles using the same number of square centimetres.
- Find the area of shapes by counting whole and half square centimetres.
- Use an overlay grid marked with square centimetres to find the areas of objects.
- Find the areas of irregular shapes.

- Use a folded-paper right angle to identify acute and obtuse angles.
- Use a plumb-line to identify vertical surfaces and edges.
- Use a spirit level to identify horizontal surfaces and edges.
- Use a folded-paper right angle or set-square to identify perpendicular lines and edges.

- Construct two-dimensional shapes using ruler, compasses and protractor, given the lengths of sides and/or sizes of angles.
- Construct skeleton models of three-dimensional shapes using straws and pipe-cleaners.
- Construct three-dimensional shapes from nets.

- Introduce rotational symmetry by rotating a shape within its outline.
- Investigate the rotational symmetry of two-dimensional shapes.

- Use coordinates to identify or plot the position of a point on a square grid.
- Use coordinates to identify the position of a square within a square grid.
- Use six-figure grid references to identify or plot the position of a point which lies within a square on a square grid.
- Use bearings to identify or plot the direction of an object.
- Use bearings and distances to identify or plot the position of an object.

Level 4 : attainment targets 1–7

Use this chart to check which attainment targets are covered by each activity.

ACTIVITY	1			2						3			4			5		6		7
	A	B	C	A	B	C	D	E	F	A	B	C	A	B	C	A	B	A	B	
Energy	▲	▲	•	•	•	•			•	•	•	•	•	•						
Sports day	•	•																		
Disco	•	•			•	•	•	•		•	•	▲	•	•	•					
Best buys	•	•	•	•	•	•			•	•	•	▲	•	•	•					
Packaging	•																			
Litter	•	•	•				•	•		•	•	•	•	•						
Traffic survey		•		•																
Buses	•	•					•	•												
Land use	•	•					•	▲												
Maths walks	•	•		•			•	•	•											
Minibeasts	•	•				•														
The spread of a tree	•	•	•																	
Testing materials	▲	•																		
Testing structures	•	•																		
Computer games	•	•		•													•			
Studying the past	•	•	•																	
Number systems				•	•				▲	•	•					•	•			
Turtle geometry			•																	
Fenced in	•	•																		
How many squares?	•	•	•														▲	•		
Diagonals	•	•	•													•	▲	•		
Bounce	•	•	•														▲	•		
Throwing a die							•													
All aboard		•	•								•					•	▲	•		
Hexagons																				
Constructing houses	•																			
Religious symbols							•	•		•	•	•	•	•						
Four-by-four																				▲
Along the dragon's back										•									▲	
Beat the goalie										•				▲	▲					
Polyominoes																				
Badminton										▲				•						

Key: • = touches on
▲ = especially
relevant

Level 4 : attainment targets 8–14

Use this chart to check which attainment targets are covered by each activity.

ACTIVITY	8A	8B	8C	9A	9B	9C	10A	10B	11A	11B	12A	12B	12C	13A	13B	13C	13D	14A	14B	14C
Energy	●		●	●	●	●					●	●	●	●	●	●				
Sports day	●		●	●	●						●	●	●	●	●	●				
Disco				●	●	●					●			●	●	●				
Best buys				●	●	●					●	●	●	●						
Packaging	●	●	●	●	●	●		▲			●	●		●						
Litter			●	▲	▲	●					●	●		●		●			●	
Traffic survey											●	●	▲	●		●				
Buses				●	●	●						●		●	●	●				
Land use		▲		●	●	●							●							
Maths walks			●	▲	▲		●	●	●		●		●	●						
Minibeasts			●	●	●						●		●	▲		●				
The spread of a tree	▲	●	●	●	●		●													
Testing materials	●		●	▲	●						●	●		●		●				
Testing structures	●		●	●	●	●					●	●		●		●				
Computer games											●		●					●	●	
Studying the past				●	●															
Number systems																				
Turtle geometry						●	●	●	▲											
Fenced in		▲						●								●				
How many squares?																●				
Diagonals																●				
Bounce							●									●				
Throwing a die					●	●					●	●					●	▲	▲	▲
All aboard																				
Hexagons										●										
Constructing houses	●			●				▲								●				
Religious symbols							●	●	▲											
Four-by-four									●											
Along the dragon's back																				
Beat the goalie																				
Polyominoes		●							▲	●										
Badminton																				

Key: ● = touches on
    ▲ = especially relevant

Level 4 : Contexts

This chart shows the wider contexts of each activity.

ACTIVITY	Everyday situations	Everyday problems	Games and fun	Maths problems	Maths investigations	Calculator activities	Computer activities	English (Core)	Science (Core)	Art (Foundation)	PE	History	Geography	Music	Technology	Local Curriculum	RE	Possible topic link	School-wide themes
Energy	•	•				•			•						•	•		•	
Sports day	•	•									•								
Disco	•	•				•				•									
Best buys	•					•	•											•	•
Packaging									•	•					•	•		•	•
Litter	•	•											•			•		•	
Traffic survey	•	•											•			•			•
Buses	•					•	•						•			•			•
Land use							•			•		•	•			•		•	
Maths walks					•			•	•	•			•			•		•	•
Minibeasts							•	•	•										
The spread of a tree									•									•	
Testing materials									•						•			•	
Testing structures									•						•			•	
Computer games				•	•		•												
Studying the past						•	•	•				•	•					•	
Number systems					•					•		•	•				•	•	
Turtle geometry				•			•						•						
Fenced in					•	•													
How many squares?					•		•												
Diagonals					•														
Bounce			•		•		•												
Throwing a die			•		•		•												
All aboard				•															
Hexagons					•					•									
Constructing houses										•						•		•	
Religious symbols					•												•	•	
Four-by-four			•		•														
Along the dragon's back			•			•													
Beat the goalie			•		•	•													
Polyominoes			•																
Badminton			•			•													

Chapter five
Level 5

Introduction

Mathematical activities at this level can help children to come to terms with their own increasing responsibility for themselves and for other people. Many children will have little or no experience of balancing a budget or handling money sensibly, and mathematics can provide a good way of introducing these concepts and showing their importance.

Children will grow in experience if they participate in the planning of educational visits. This can lead not only to an increased mathematical fluency but also to a more mature understanding of the problems involved in organisation and their solutions.

Children at Level 5 will be introduced to networks and the problems they can solve, and they will also be involved in more sophisticated exercises in probability.

The mathematical problems and games suggested for this level are increasingly open-ended, and they can often be solved by more than one method. Children will benefit from encouragement to experiment with possible solutions and develop their own ways of tackling problems.

Planning a visit

Educational visits will no doubt continue in spite of the uncertainties raised by recent legislation. Schools will still value the contribution which such visits make to the child's educational, social and personal development. Teachers will therefore be trying to overcome difficulties and ensure that visits can continue to take place.

Considering the skills and ideas which children have acquired by this stage, they are ready to undertake a large share in the planning of visits. Here is an example of the extent to which children can be involved in planning their stay. This example refers to a residential visit, though a number of the activities are relevant to non-residential outings.

Making arrangements

The children were given the task of organising a five-day visit to a field centre near a partner school, so they could engage in joint activities.

Different groups were given responsibility for certain areas such as transport, leisure activities and catering arrangements. This is a record of the efforts of the catering group, showing how their activities matched statements at Level 5.

Menus

First the group made a list of food which would be both convenient and nutritious. The class were then surveyed for likes and dislikes, and mealtime groups were drawn up on the basis of this, keeping friends together as far as possible.

Group menus were planned taking account of the preferences of the different groups, and in some instances there were separate menus for individuals.

With the assistance of the catering staff at the school, and using their own observations and measurements, the catering group estimated the amounts of food they would need to buy.

Stores near the school and the destination were then contacted, and food prices compared.

The children concluded that although it would be more convenient to place an order with a shop near their destination (which could be collected on arrival) the additional cost of most items made this an expensive option.

The children were reluctant to compromise on quality and quantity in order to afford the prices of the shop near their destination, so they compromised by purchasing most of the food locally and phoning through to the other store a smaller order for items which would not travel well.

The children also organised cooking, cleaning and tidying rotas.

During the visit no emergency trips were made to the local 'chippie' – a testimony to the success of the group's efforts!

Essential language
Survey, percentage, estimate.

ATs 1AB, 3B, 4B, 8BC, 12A.

Create a game

An integral part of the children's games lesson could be the design or creation of their own games.

Give the children limitations within which to work. These restrictions will probably include the size of the court, pitch or target area for the game, and they might be dictated by the children, by you, or by the lack of space in the hall or gymnasium.

There is scope for plenty of practical mathematics work here, measuring and selecting the appropriate materials. The task can involve measuring areas,

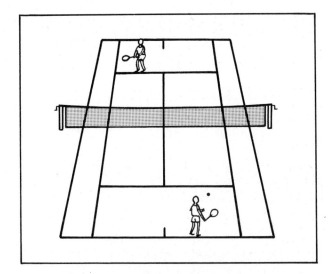

perimeters, circumferences and diameters.

One game might demand the design of a court to cover an area of 36 square metres, or to have a certain perimeter or diameter.

Working in small groups, the children can be involved in planning the most economical use of the available space to accommodate as many children as possible.

Essential language
Measure, measurement, metres, decimal notation, area, perimeter, circumference, diameter, plan, scale.

ATs 1AB, 4A, 8AC.

Fitness

PE can be an enjoyable and rewarding topic of study. While discovering about their physical abilities, children will be using a range of mathematical skills.

Here are some activities in which the children can assess their fitness, and make comparisons with other people.
• What happens to pulse-rate, breathing and reactions after:
  testing speed over short distances;
  testing speed over longer distances;
  testing how many hops can be made on and off a bench in a minute? (If pulse and breathing rates are taken at two- or three-minute intervals after exercise, a line graph will show the falling-off as these rates return to normal.)
• Test leg strength when pushing and pulling.

- Test arm strength when pushing and pulling.
- Find out the capacity of different people's lungs.

In planning such investigations, the children will have to select the correct materials and mathematics for the task.

The tasks themselves will demand accurate use of a range of measuring instruments and units.

Recording and presenting the results will challenge the children's capacity to select, organise and compare material, including the creation or use of a database. There will also be opportunities for calculating the mean and range of a set of data.

Essential language
Mean, range, data, metre, centimetre, kilogram, gram.

ATs 1A, 8C, 9AB, 12ABC, 13BC.

In the news

Just how aware are the children of what is happening in the world around them? A number of activities can be generated from an investigation into current affairs, and at this level the children will be able to plan much of the investigation.

One possible activity would be to do a news-awareness survey in the school.
- How many out of a selected number of current major news items are children aware of?
- Is there any correlation between the age of the children and their awareness of the news?
- Which sorts of news items are best known to children?
- From which of the media forms do children obtain news?
Radio: Which station? Local or national?
Television: Which channel? Which programmes or bulletins?
Newspapers: Which papers? Local or national?
- What proportion of children's listening, viewing or reading time involves finding out about what is happening in the world around?

Such a survey could be linked to a wider study of the media:
- Which is the most popular mass medium?
- Which newspaper do most of the children's parents read?
- Which is the most popular radio station?
- During which periods of the day is the radio listened to most?
- Which is the most popular TV channel?
- Which are the most popular periods of the day for watching television?

There are a number of similar activities providing contexts for the gathering, interpretation and presentation of data which also require careful preparation and organisation of ideas and material.

Essential language
Data, collate, analyse, survey, continuous data, equal class intervals, frequency table, grouped data, diagram.

ATs 1B, 3B, 9AB, 12AB, 13AC.

146

Family budgets

Ask a group of children to feed the following households for a week, working within their budgets, planning the meals and finding out the current prices of the foods.

- 24 Lilac Road – Mrs Snell, OAP; £14
- 26 Lilac Road – Ms Arthur and daughter Claire, aged 2; £20
- 28 Lilac Road – Mr and Mrs Norman and their children Tom, aged 11, and Sally, aged 8; £45
- 30 Lilac Road – Mr Benson; £25

Familiarising children with planning finances and working within the constraints of a budget can help them to come to terms with increasing responsibilities and independence. It can also provide an insight into the difficulties some groups and individuals have in working within budgets, probably having to make compromises in the quality or quantity of food which they can buy.

If the children have already undertaken studies into nutrition, then attempting to feed the families within their respective budgets will involve a number of interesting group decisions as to what compromises they are prepared to make.

Using and applying their knowledge and understanding of percentages the children could break down the costs of various constituents of the weekly diets to see what proportion of the budgets were being spent on such things as:

- Basic foods such as bread and milk.
- Inessentials such as crisps and biscuits.
- Dairy products.
- Cereal products.
- Protein-rich products.

Essential language
Pie chart, data, percentage, fraction.

ATs 1AB, 3ABD, 4B, 9AB, 13A.

Off the shelf

The price we pay when we buy things from supermarkets reflects the overheads and profits of those involved at the various stages of bringing the food to the shelves. This pie-chart represents the percentage of the total cost due to those involved in getting an orange to the supermarket shelves.

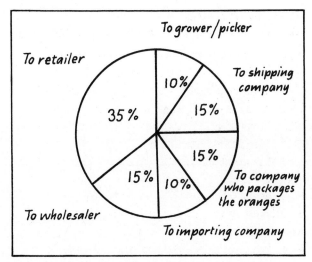

Using this information children could calculate the share of the cost which goes to each group when an orange costs 12p, 15p, 16p or 20p. In many instances these calculations will result in decimal places, which will have to be approximated to a specified number of places.

Ready reckoners in the form of conversion graphs could be constructed which would enable the children to calculate the amounts due to involved parties from a number of imported fruits and vegetables retailing at a variety of prices.

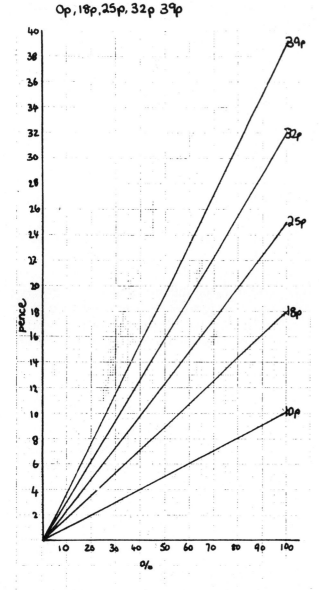

Conversion graph for calculating different percentage shares of goods costing

0p, 18p, 25p, 32p, 39p

(y-axis: pence; x-axis: %)

Miles per gallon

The fuel consumption of different cars provides a context for the construction and interpretation of conversion graphs. The following example compares some of the models made by a major company.

Model	MILES PER GALLON		
	at a constant 56 m.p.h.	at a constant 75 m.p.h.	simulated urban driving
FIESTA 1·2	57·6 mpg	40·9 mpg	44·8 mpg
ESCORT 1·3	62·8 mpg	45·6 mpg	44·1 mpg
ORION 1·4	60·1 mpg	46·3 mpg	34·9 mpg
SIERRA 1·6	51·4 mpg	39·8 mpg	31·7 mpg
GRANADA 2·0	45·6 mpg	36·7 mpg	26·2 mpg

The children could contact car dealers themselves to collect the information they need. The graphs will enable them to make comparisons between different makes and models.

Garages use both gallons and litres on petrol pumps at the moment, and these conversion graphs offer an ideal way of becoming familiar with metric measures and their Imperial equivalents.

In making these calculations, children may begin to appreciate some of the complexities involved in obtaining the things we take for granted. They will also see the relatively small proportion of the cost of foodstuffs which often goes to the producer, which may in part explain the low standard of living of many communities in the Third World.

Essential language

Fraction, percentage, approximate, pie chart, conversion graph, horizontal, vertical, axis, values.

ATs 1AB, 3B, 4B, 13A.

148

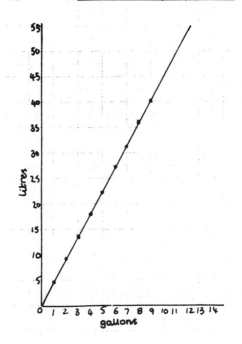

Conversion graph for gallons and litres

gallons	1	2	3	4	5	6	7	8	9
litres	4·5	9·1	13·6	18·2	22·7	27·3	31·8	36·4	40·9

The graphs can help children to tackle a number of problems; how many gallons or litres of fuel are required for journeys of different lengths? This will be of relevance around holiday times, and will give children practice with using maps. It will also extend their knowledge of unitary ratios.

Variation

This type of activity could be extended to include selecting the best or shortest route between places, perhaps from the local area to various seaside resorts or ports.

Essential language

Gallon, litre, miles, kilometres, miles per gallon (mpg), kilometres per litre (km/l), fuel consumption, distance, scale, route.

ATs 1AB, 2B, 4B, 8AB, 12A, 13B.

Old money and measures

Any study of recent social history will provide children with information which refers to pre-decimal coinage and Imperial units of measurement. Take, for example, the following family budget of an urban semi-skilled worker with three children in 1841, earning 15 shillings a week:

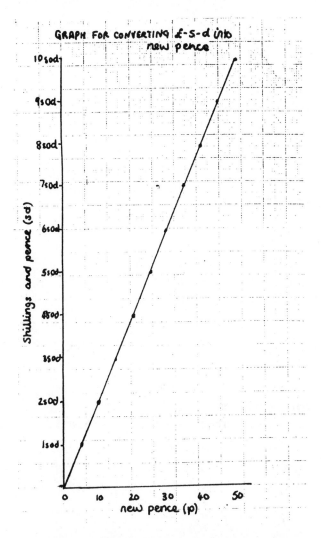

	£	s	d
5 x 4 lb. loaves at 8½ d.		3	6½
5 lb. meat at 5d. per lb.		2	1
7 pints porter at 2d. per pint		1	2
½ cwt. coals			9½
40 lb. potatoes		1	4
3 oz. tea . 1 lb. sugar		1	6
1 lb. butter			9
½ lb. soap . ½ lb. candles			6½
rent		2	6
schooling			4
other things			5½
		15	0

Source: *Finding Out About Victorian Towns*, M. Rawcliffe (Batsford).

To help children understand such information, draw up conversion graphs to convert pounds, shillings and pence to ·decimal coinage and pounds to kilograms.

Budgets could also be examined in terms of the percentage of the family income that was spent on food, rent, household items etc, and pie charts could be drawn to represent this information.

Essential language

Pound (£), shilling (s), penny (d), pound (lb), hundredweight (cwt), ounce (oz), pint (pt), kilogram (kg), gram (g), litre (l). millilitre (ml), convert, percentage.

ATs 1AB, 3B, 4B, 8BC, 9AB, 13AB.

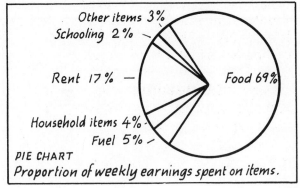

Digit shift

The calculator is a most powerful piece of equipment; it can generate a large quantity of examples very quickly. This can be of great help to children in discovering number patterns and relationships. An understanding of numbers is crucial to the ability to do mental arithmetic, and the calculator plays an additional role initially by relieving the child of the burden of calculation, allowing attention to be focused on the recognition of pattern. Once this has been established, the calculator will become superfluous.

Here is an example of this kind of calculator-generated activity.

4 x 100 = ___	40 x 100 = ___	40 x 300 = ___
		40 x 500 = ___
		40 x 700 = ___
		40 x 900 = ___
6 x 100 = ___	60 x 100 = ___	60 x 300 = ___
		60 x 500 = ___
		60 x 700 = ___
		60 x 900 = ___

Ask the children to use a calculator to find answers to these and similar sorts of number questions.

What do they notice?

Varied examples of this sort can give rise to many different and interesting number patterns.

Essential language
Multiply, divide, ten, hundred, thousand, ten thousand, digit, column, multiples, powers.

ATs 1B, 3C, 5C.

LOGO activities

Using LOGO, one way of moving the turtle around the screen is by specifying its location by means of coordinates in the four quadrants.

Moving turtles
Using just two numbers you can always describe the position of the turtle on the screen. These numbers are called the x and y coordinates. Imagine the x-axis going from side to side and the y-axis going up and down. The mid-point of the screen is 0 on both the axes. Points to the left, on the x-axis, are negative, with a minus sign, and points to the right are positive, with a plus sign. Points above the mid point are positive on the y-axis, and points below are negative.

By entering the x and y coordinates in LOGO you can move the turtle; you can also get the computer to state the turtle's position by means of the coordinates.

Islamic patterns
Islamic patterns are both intricate and beautiful. They can provide a variety of starting points for exploring pattern, shape and tessellations using the turtle.
- The first step in reproducing the design by means of the floor turtle is to look closely at the pattern you are thinking about.
- See if you can spot a simple basic shape that repeats to generate the overall pattern.

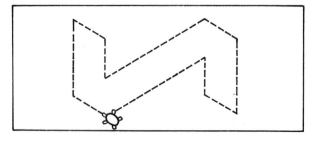

- Isolate that shape and consider its format.
- If it looks too complicated, break it up into smaller parts.
- Attempt to define LOGO procedures to draw these simpler shapes, and then try to construct your overall solution using these procedures as building blocks.

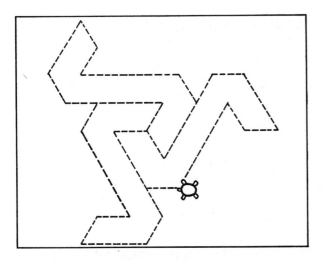

In order to repeat the basic shape, you may need to develop another procedure for the turtle. Then by writing further procedures the pattern can be extended.

Many patterns can be generated in this way, and a similar thought-process could easily be adapted for producing Islamic patterns manually on paper.

Essential language

x and y coordinates, x-axis tessellation. y-axis, negative, positive.

ATs 3D, 4A, 6B, 7, 10AB, 11AC.

Tessellation

Experimenting with tessellations of triangles and quadrilaterals helps illustrate the geometrical properties of the shapes involved.

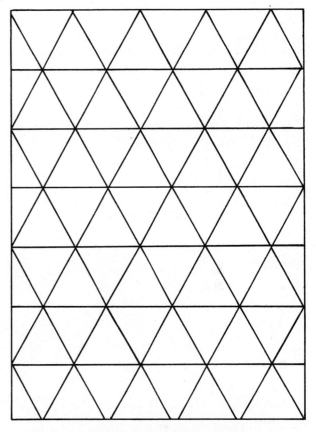

The tessellation of triangles illustrated shows the following properties of triangles:
● Congruent triangles, those which have the same shape and size, will tessellate on their own.
● The three angles of a triangle add up to 180 degrees.
● The diagram illustrates that the corresponding angles A and C are equal, as are the adjacent angles A and B.

There are many more patterns which can emerge from making tessellations; the children can experiment with regular and irregular polygons of all sorts.

Essential language

Tessellate, triangle, equilateral, isosceles, scalene, right-angled, quadrilateral, rhombus, parallelogram, trapezium, kite, congruent, similar, parallel, corresponding angle, adjacent angle.

ATs 10AB, 11A.

Mystic roses

'Mystic roses' is an investigation which uses and applies mathematics in various ways, and introduces the need to express simple functions symbolically.

This activity is concerned with investigating the number of diagonals in regular polygons. A diagonal of a polygon in this case is taken to be a straight line which connects any two vertices (corners) which are not adjacent.

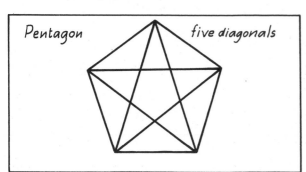

Pentagon   five diagonals

What you need
Paper, pencils, rulers.

What to do
The children have to investigate the number of diagonals in different regular polygons in order to attempt to discover a relationship which connects the number of sides of the polygon with the number of its diagonals.

Encourage the children to work methodically and to keep careful records of each of their examples so that they will have enough information on which to base their generalisations of the relationship.

sides	diagonals
3	0
4	2
5	5
6	9

The relationship which the children are looking for is as follows:

The number of diagonals in a polygon with n sides is given by

$$\frac{n(n-3)}{2}$$

This investigation is also available as a computer program, *Polygon*. The program includes a three-question test for children who think they may have discovered the relationship.

Polygon is available from MUSE, PO Box 43, Hull, HU1 2HD.

Essential language
Investigate, relationship, generalise, polygon, vertices, diagonals, adjacent.

ATs 1ABC, 5BC, 6AB, 11A.

The sieve of Eratosthenes

A prime number is a number which is divisible only by itself and one. An easy way to find all the primes between one and 100 is known as 'the sieve of Eratosthenes'.

What you need
A 100 square with the numbers filled in.

What to do
First, put a circle round the number 1 on the 100 square.

Put a circle round 2, then colour every multiple of 2.

Put a circle round 3, then colour every multiple of 3.

4 will already be coloured in.

Put a circle round 5, then colour every multiple of 5.

6 will already be coloured in.

Put a circle round 7, then colour every multiple of 7.

Then progress through the 100 square in this way until every square containing a number is either coloured in or circled round.

All the circled numbers are prime numbers.

Essential language
Factors, prime numbers, 100 square, multiple, divisible, product.

ATs 1ABC, 5ABC.

Polygonal numbers

This investigation will provide children with experience of the number patterns which arise through spatial arrangements. To develop polygonal numbers, dots are arranged to make a sequence of similar polygons, the length of whose sides increases by one unit each time. The first four terms of the sequence of triangular, square, pentagonal and hexagonal numbers are shown below:

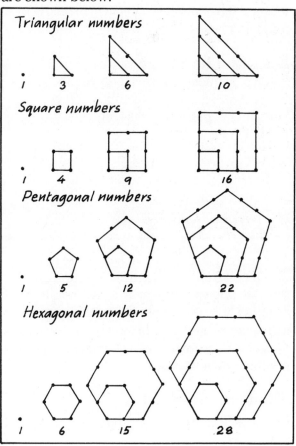

What you need
Copies of the polygonal numbers diagrams for each child.

What to do
Ask the children to explore and continue the patterns shown on the diagrams. They could list the numbers produced in each of the sequences, and explore the differences between each successive term.

Can the children generalise each pattern? Ask them if they can find a way of continuing each pattern without drawing any new diagrams.

Variation
Suggest the following activities to the children:
• Can you find out the heptagonal (seven-sided) numbers without drawing diagrams?
• Can you discover a relationship between triangular numbers and square numbers? (Adding two successive triangular numbers produces a square number.)
• Can you discover a relationship that connects triangular and pentagonal numbers with square numbers? (Adding triangular and pentagonal numbers whose terms are the same gives twice a square number.)

Essential language
Pattern, sequence, terms, polygonal, triangular, square, pentagonal, hexagonal, heptagonal, pattern of difference, relationship.

ATs 1ABC, 5ABC.

Regular polygons

This activity provides a useful context in which children can practise measuring and drawing angles to the nearest degree. It requires the correct use of drawing instruments, and also provides an opportunity for the division of three-digit numbers in context.

What you need
Rulers, protractors, pencils, pairs of compasses.

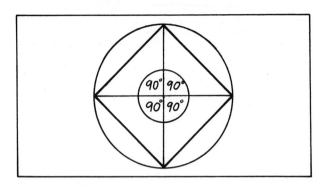

What to do
This method of constructing regular polygons within a circle is rather like drawing the spokes of a wheel. For example, to draw a square, which has four corners, we need to draw four equally-spaced 'spokes' and as 360 divided by four is 90, the angle between each spoke should be 90 degrees.

Ask the children whether it is necessary to measure each angle. In fact, only one angle need be measured, as the compasses can be set to the distance between the two points where the arms of the angle cut the circumference of the circle. The compasses are then used to 'step off' the other corners of the polygon around the circumference.

Ask the children to devise a rule or formula for finding out the size of the angle to be measured when constructing any regular polygon.

(This could be represented as:
$$a = \frac{360}{n}$$
where 'a' represents the size of the angle and 'n' represents the number of corners in the polygon.)

Essential language
Protractor, compasses, degrees, circumference, radius, rule, formula, construct.

ATs 6AB, 8D, 10B, 11A.

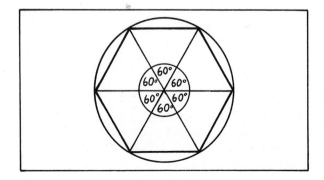

Transformations

These activities give children experience with the use of coordinates in four quadrants, and with the identification of the types of symmetry possessed by various shapes.

Translations and reflections

All the stages of this activity are shown in Figure 1.

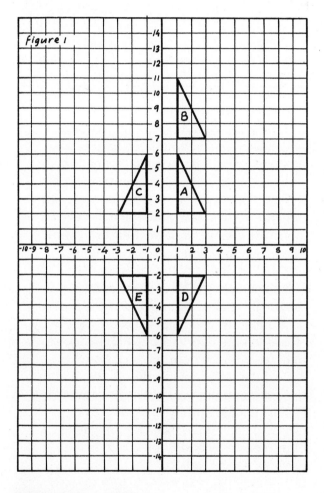

What you need

Squared paper, tracing paper, pencils, rulers.

What to do

• On squared paper, draw an x-axis from −10 to +10 and a y-axis from −12 to +12.
• Plot these points in order: (1, 2) (1, 6) (3, 2), then join the points to form triangle A. Make a tracing of triangle A to help with the transformation questions which follow.
• Add five to the second coordinate of each pair, plot these points and join to form triangle B. What transformation does the move A → B show?
(*A translation*).
• Using the coordinates of triangle A, change the sign (+ or −) of the first coordinate in each pair, plot these points and join them to form triangle C. What transformation does the move A → C show?
(*A reflection in the vertical axis*).
• Again using the coordinates of triangle A, change the sign of the second coordinate in each set, plot these points and join as before to produce triangle D. What transformation is shown by the move A → D?
(*A reflection in the horizontal axis*).
• Finally, starting with the coordinates for triangle A, change the signs of both coordinates in each pair, plot these points and join to form triangle E. What transformation is demonstrated by the move C → E?
(*A reflection in the horizontal axis*).

Rotations

The stages of this activity are shown in Figure 2.

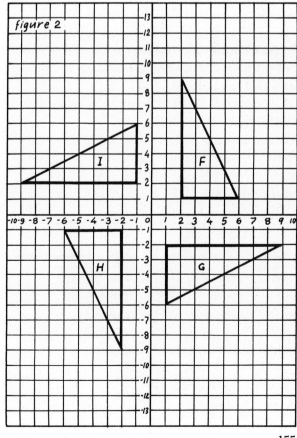

What you need
Squared paper, tracing paper, rulers, pencils.

What to do
● On squared paper, draw an x-axis from −10 to 10 and a y-axis from −10 to +10.
● Plot these points in order; (2, 1) (2, 9) (6, 1), then join them to produce triangle F.
● Make a tracing of the axes of the graph and the position of triangle F to help with the next stages of the activity.
● Rotate triangle F through 90°, plot its new position and label this as triangle G. List the coordinates of triangle G.
● Next, rotate triangle F through 180°, plot its new position and label as triangle H. List the coordinates of triangle H.
● Finally, rotate triangle F through 270°, plot its new position and label this as triangle I. List the coordinates of triangle I.
● Compare the coordinates of triangle F with the coordinates of triangles G, H and I. Can you recognise a pattern in the coordinates?

In fact, from F → G (90° rotation) each pair of the coordinates of F is reversed and the sign of the resulting second coordinate in each pair is changed.

From F → H (180° rotation) the sign of each coordinate of F is changed.

From F → I (270° rotation) each pair of the coordinates of F is reversed and the sign of the resulting first coordinate in each pair is changed.

Essential language
Horizontal axis, vertical axis, x-axis, y-axis, axes, negative, positive, plot, points, position, coordinates, transformation, translation, reflection, rotation.

ATs 7, 10A, 11AC.

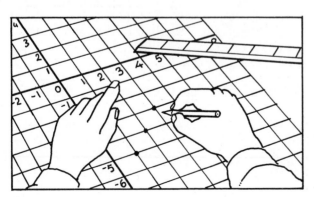

Channel crossing

Here is a problem which should produce a great deal of discussion about the use and application of mathematics.

What you need
A copy of the map illustrated for each child (See also page 186).

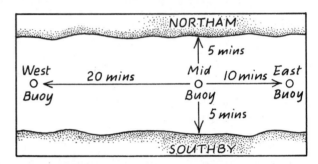

What to do
Using the map of a busy imaginary channel or estuary, the children have to plan a timetable for a ferry service taking into account other shipping movements. The ferry crosses the channel in a north-south direction, whilst other shipping travels along the channel in a west-east direction. The problem which is presented below may be tackled in many different ways.

If ships pass the West Buoy at five-minute intervals beginning at two minutes past the hour, and ships pass the East Buoy at five-minute intervals beginning at four minutes past the hour, at what times should the ferry sail in order to make the maximum number of crossings between Northam and Southby, making a safe crossing each time? The shipping lanes cross very near Mid Buoy which is the obvious danger zone.

TIMES AT WHICH SHIPS PASS WEST AND EAST BUOYS	
	Minutes past each hour
West Buoy	02.07.12.17.22.27.32.37.42.47.52.57
East Buoy	04.09.14.19.24.29.34.39.44.49.54.59

TIMES AT WHICH SHIPS REACH MID BUOY	
	Minutes past each hour
From West Buoy	22.27.32.37.42.47.52.57.02.07.12.17
From East Buoy	14.19.24.29.34.39.44.49.54.59.04.09

The problem may be worked in the following way:
- First, work out the times at which ships pass both West and East Buoys.
- Then find the times at which these ships will reach Mid Buoy.
- This will indicate the 'danger times' to be avoided by the ferry, and also the 'safe times' for the ferry to pass Mid Buoy.
- As the ferry takes five minutes to reach Mid Buoy from either side of the channel, the safe departure times for the ferry can be found by working back from the identified 'safe times'.

SAFE TIMES FOR THE FERRY AT MID BUOY AND FERRY DEPARTURE TIMES	
	Minutes past each hour
'Safe' times at Mid Buoy.	00.01.03.05.06.08.10.11.13.15.16.18 etc
Ferry departure times.	55.56.58.00.01.03.05.06.08.10.11.13 etc

In this case the times that the ships pass each of the buoys can be expressed in the following algebraic form:
- Ships passing West Buoy $t=5x-3$, where 't' represents the time the ship passes the buoy and 'x' represents the order in which the ship left East Buoy.
- Ships passing East Buoy $t=5x-1$.

The times that these ships reach Mid Buoy can also be expressed algebraically as below:
- Ships from West Buoy $t=(5x-3)+20$, where 't' represents the time the ship reaches Mid Buoy.
- Ships from East Buoy $t=(5x-1)+10$.

Children who seem good at finding solutions could be encouraged to develop their own variations.

Variation
Extend this problem by including additional variables such as the distances between buoys and the speed of the ships.

In order to attempt this it may assist teachers to know that the speed of ships is measured in knots, one knot being a speed of one nautical mile per hour (approximately 1.15 mph.).

Essential language
Algebra, variables.

ATs 1ABC, 4A, 5C, 6AB, 8A.

Networks

The following activities should provide children with experiences which will develop their ability to solve problems using networks.

Traversability

What you need
Copies of different networks, such as those illustrated.

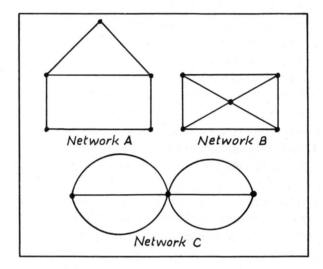
Network A   Network B
Network C

What to do
Ask the children to try to draw over all the lines of each network without taking their pencils off the paper and without drawing over any of the lines more than once. This will indicate whether or not each network is traversable.

Ask the children whether they can discover a rule which would tell them whether a network is traversable.
Introduce the following terms:
- Arc – a line on a network.
- Node – a point on a network where arcs meet.
- Odd node – a node where an odd number of arcs meet.
- Even node – a node where an even number of arcs meet.

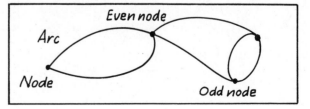
Even node
Arc
Node
Odd node

Ask the children to copy and complete this table for the networks they have tried:

Network	Number of odd nodes	Number of even nodes	Is the network traversable?
A	2	3	yes
B	4	1	no
C	2	1	yes

When they have completed their tables, ask the following questions:
- Is a network with more than two even nodes traversable?
- Is a network with more than two odd nodes traversable?
- Can you suggest a rule which will tell us whether a network is traversable?

The rule which the children are being asked to find is that which was first discovered by the Swiss mathematician Leonhard Euler (1707–83), which states that a network is not traversable if it contains more than two odd nodes, as the odd nodes in any network must be used as either starting or finishing points for traversing the network.

The bridges of Königsberg

This famous problem is the one which led Euler into making his study of traversable networks. Königsberg at the time was in Germany (it is now known as Kaliningrad and is in the USSR). It was a town built on two islands and on the banks of the River Pregel. The islands and the river banks were connected by seven bridges, and for many years the people of the town had tried to find a way of starting from one point in the town, crossing every bridge once and then returning to their starting place.

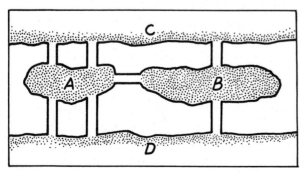

What you need
Copies of the map illustrated.

What to do
Provide the children with a copy of the map and ask them to try to solve the problem.

In his examination of the problem, Euler represented the map as a network like that shown below, which may help in the children's work.

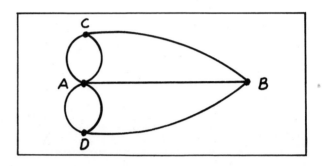

Euler realised that the key to the problem lay in the fact that five arcs met at node A, and three each at nodes B, C and D, so there were four odd nodes. He went on to show that an odd node could only be a starting or finishing point for traversing the network, so the Königsberg problem could not be solved as the network contained more than two odd nodes.

When the children have discovered that this problem cannot be solved, ask them how the people of Königsberg could change their bridges in order that they may solve the problem. Two possible solutions to this are shown below:

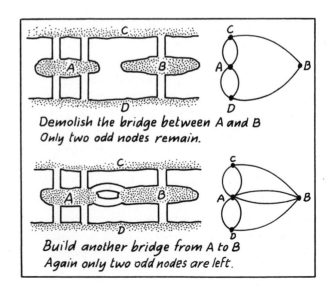

Demolish the bridge between A and B
Only two odd nodes remain.

Build another bridge from A to B
Again only two odd nodes are left.

Watchperson

Watchperson is a computer program involving network traversing problems. It is available from Tecmedia, in the MEP Microprimer 3 pack.

What you need
Access to a computer and the program, or pencil and paper and copies of the town plans.

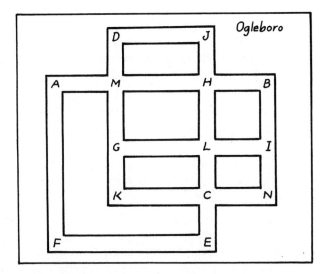

What to do
As the watchperson, it is the player's job to patrol the streets of one of three imaginary towns, Ogleboro, Kunktown or Lindberg. The job varies in difficulty according to which town is being patrolled.

The task of the watchperson is to walk all the streets of the town without retracing his or her footsteps. Although the watchperson may not walk twice on any street, corners may be revisited. The child is asked to choose the letter of the junction (node) they wish to start from and then the direction in which they wish to move, either north, south, east or west. Each time a junction is reached, the child has to choose the direction of the next move. The program continues in this way until either all the streets have been patrolled successfully or a mistake has been made.

Children working away from the computer could be provided with duplicated maps of the three towns so they can plan the route to be taken when they use the program. The whole activity could of course be done without a computer in this way.

The children could also be asked to create their own maps of imaginary towns and then give these to their partners to solve. It is important here to remind the children that their maps should have no more than two odd nodes.

The paperboy's round

This is a problem which uses networks to discover the shortest possible route. Consider the following problem:

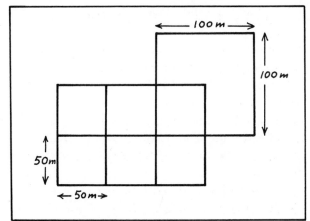

The map illustrated shows the streets which are on the paperboy's round. The length of each side of a small square represents 50 metres. What is the shortest distance that the paperboy can walk in order to complete his round?

What you need
Copies of the map.

What to do
Give the children copies of the map, and ask them to find the total length of all the streets (in this case 1150m or 1.15km).

Next, ask the children to try to solve the problem using their knowledge of networks. Some may realise that the network is not traversable.

If the map is represented as a network it can be seen that the nodes at B, D, F and G are odd and all the rest are even. So the network is not traversable, as there are more than two odd nodes.

This means that if the paperboy walks a street between two odd nodes twice, then the rest of the streets can be walked along once only. As D and G are the two odd nodes which are closest together, the paperboy walks twice along the street between them. This leaves two other odd nodes at B and F, which must be used as starting and finishing points.

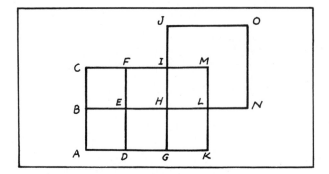

Ask the children if they can see why it is necessary to start and finish at B and F.

As the paperboy has to walk twice along the street between D and G, he walks 50 metres longer than the total length of all the streets, or 1200m (1.2km) in all.

One possible route that the paperboy may take is:
B-E-F-I-J-O-N-L-M-I-H-L-K-G-H-E-D-G-A-B-C-F

Ask the children to construct their own problems of this kind, or provide them with other examples.

Networks and regions

This is an investigation into the relationship between the number of arcs, nodes and regions in a network. The regions of a network are the 'spaces' between the arcs and also include the region outside the network.

What you need
Copies of a sheet showing various networks.

What to do
Present the children with a duplicated sheet of different networks. For each network ask them to count the number of arcs, nodes and regions, not forgetting to count the region outside the network. Get the children to record their discoveries on a table.

When the table of results is complete, ask the children to compare the number of

160

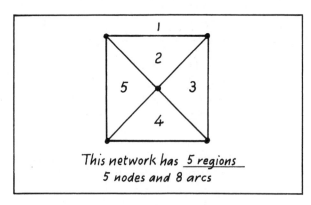

This network has __5 regions__
5 nodes and 8 arcs

nodes and regions in each network with the number of arcs. As a further clue, suggest that they add together the numbers of nodes and regions for each network and then compare this total with the number of arcs. The children should realise that the number of nodes plus the number of regions is always two greater than the number of arcs. This relationship may be represented algebraically as: $n+r-a=2$, where 'n' represents the number of nodes, 'r' the number of regions and 'a' the number of arcs.

Test this relationship by giving the children problems such as this: 'If a network has five nodes and seven arcs, how many regions must it have?'

Verify their solutions by drawing the network.

Sprouts

'Sprouts' is a network game for two players.

What you need
Pencil and paper.

What to do
Start by marking three points at random on the paper. These become the nodes of a network as the game continues.

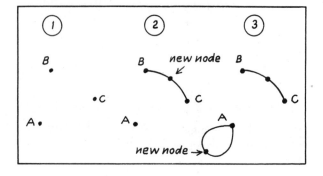

The first player then joins any two nodes with an arc and marks a new node in the middle of the arc so drawn.

Alternatively, the player may draw an arc so that it begins and ends at the same node, again marking a new node in the middle of the arc.

The next player continues the game by adding another arc to the network, again marking a new node in the middle of the arc. Play continues in this way with each player in turn drawing a new arc and marking a node in the middle of the arc, providing neither of these two rules are broken:

• no more than three arcs can join any one node,

• no arc may cross itself or any other arc.

Nodes which cannot be used due to the first rule are called 'dead nodes' and are circled. The aim of the game is to prevent the other player from making a legitimate move. The last player to make a legal move wins the game. Here is an example game:

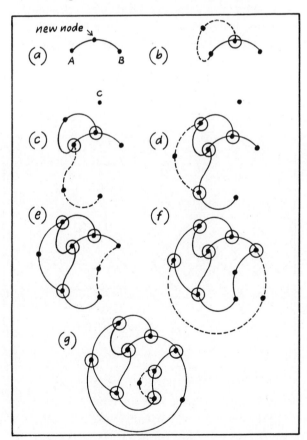

The player making the move in diagram (g) wins the game because the other player cannot draw a new arc without breaking the rules.

When the children have tried this game, ask the following questions:

• Which player is most likely to win, the first or the second player – or doesn't it make any difference? (The first player can always win, if he plays logically.)

• What is the greatest number of moves that can be made in one complete game? (In the game which begins with three nodes, the greatest number of possible moves is eight.)

• What is the least number of moves in which a game can end? (In a game beginning with three nodes, the lowest number of possible moves is six.)

The inventor of the game, Professor Conway of Cambridge University, developed a proof that any game must end in at most 3n–1 moves, where 'n' represents the number of nodes drawn at the start of the game. Each node has three 'lives' – the three arcs that may meet at that node. A node that has three arcs is called a 'dead spot' because no more arcs can be drawn to it.

A game that begins with n nodes has a starting life of 3n. Each move kills two lives, at the beginning and end of the arc, but adds a new node with a life of one. Therefore, each move decreases the total life of the game by one. Obviously, a game cannot continue when only one life remains, as at least two lives are required to make a move. Accordingly, no game can last beyond 3n–1 moves, and the least number of possible moves to end a game is 2n moves.

Variations

The children could play the game again, this time starting with two, four, or five nodes. Ask the children to consider the same questions as for the three node game.

Alternatively, try changing the rules of the game slightly so that each node is allowed to have four arcs joining it before becoming 'dead', and ask the children to investigate this variation.

Essential language

Network, traversable, arc, node, odd, even, junction, direction, route, region.

ATs 3D, 6AB, 9ABC, 11B.

Pascal's triangle

This triangular array of numbers was developed in the seventeenth century by the French philosopher and mathematician Blaise Pascal. Pascal was interested in games of chance, and the diagram shows his findings about the probabilities involved in two-state systems, such as the tossing of coins, where there are two possible outcomes on the toss of each coin. Pascal's triangle is useful both in the study of probability and in the exploration of number patterns. An interesting activity applies the triangle to situations generated by Galton's Quincunx.

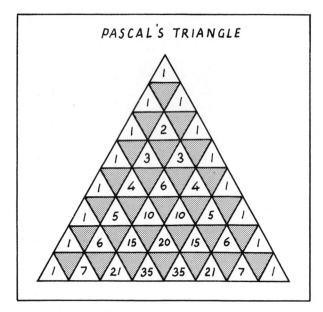

PASCAL'S TRIANGLE

What you need
Wooden board, nails, thin wooden slats, hammer, adhesive, marbles or ball-bearings, copies of Pascal's triangle, squared paper.

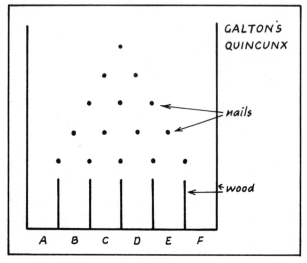

GALTON'S QUINCUNX

nails

wood

A B C D E F

What to do
Make a model of Galton's Quincunx (see illustration). This can be made easily using wood and nails, providing that the nails are spaced equally so that a marble or ball-bearing will pass easily between them.

The ball-bearings or marbles are rolled down the maze of nails so that each time they hit a nail they will go either left or right to hit one of the pins diagonally below in the next row, and so on until they come to rest in one of the channels A, B, C, D, E, or F.

Ask the children to investigate the Quincunx by rolling 32 marbles or ball-bearings down the maze, and recording how many of them come to rest in each of the channels. These results could then be shown on a graph.

Ask the children to compare their findings with those of others in the group and combine all the results of the group in order to provide a larger sample. What do they notice?
- In which channel(s) did most of the marbles finish?
- In which channel(s) did fewest of the marbles finish?
- Why?

This last question can best be demonstrated on a grid, as shown below:

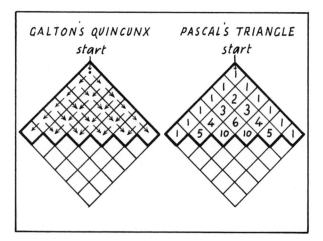

GALTON'S QUINCUNX
start

PASCAL'S TRIANGLE
start

The diagrams illustrate that starting from the top square and moving diagonally downwards there are a defined number of possible routes to every other square, the possible moves at each stage corresponding to the movement of the marble each time it strikes a nail in the Quincunx. Recording the possible moves into each square gives rise to the arrangement of numbers found in Pascal's triangle.

At this stage, the children could be asked to relate this discovery to their investigation of the Quincunx:
- What is the probability of a marble stopping in each of the channels?
- How many marbles out of 32 should ideally stop in each channel?
- How are your answers related to Pascal's triangle?

Pascal's triangle and coin tossing

What you need
Plenty of coins for tossing, squared paper, copies of Pascal's triangle.

What to do
Ask the children to investigate the probabilities involved in tossing coins, using one, two, three and then four coins, and basing their investigation on the following points:
- What are the possible outcomes?
- What is the probability of each outcome occurring?

Remind them of Cardan's formula for probability.

$$\frac{\text{number of favourable cases}}{\text{total number of cases}} \quad \frac{\text{(ways of getting desired outcome)}}{\text{(all possible outcomes)}}$$

- How many times would you expect each outcome to occur with a given number of tosses? (This has a bearing on the sum of the numbers in the corresponding row of Pascal's triangle.)
- Test your prediction by tossing the coins the given number of times and record by tallying.
- Graph both your results and your predictions. What do you notice?
- Compare your results with others in the group. What do you notice?
- Combine the results of the whole group to give a larger sample. Graph both these combined results and the ideal results on

the same graph. What do you notice?

When three coins are tossed there are four possible distinct outcomes, in eight different arrangements: all heads (HHH), two heads and one tail (HHT, HTH, THH), two tails and one head (TTH, THT, HTT) and all tails (TTT).

The probability of getting all heads or tails is 1/8, and of getting one head and two tails or one tail and two heads is 3/8.

The numbers in the fourth row of Pascal's triangle equate with the probability of tossing three coins, the first number in the row indicating all heads, the next for one less head and one more tail and so on. The sum of the numbers in the row gives the number of different arrangements of the distinct possible outcomes, in this case eight.

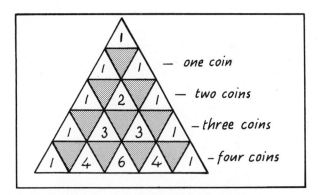

Ask the children to compare the probabilities of expected outcomes with each row of Pascal's triangle.
- What do they notice?
- Can they continue the pattern of numbers in the triangle so that they could predict the outcomes of tossing five, six and seven coins?

| Tally chart for tossing coins ten times | | |
Number of coins	Heads	Tails
1	ЖІІ ІІ	ІІІ
2	ЖІ ЖІ ІІ	ЖІ ІІІ
3	ЖІ ЖІ ЖІ ІІ	ЖІ ЖІ ІІІ
4	ЖІ ЖІ ЖІ ІІІІ	ЖІ ЖІ ЖІ ЖІ І

Number patterns in Pascal's triangle

The following diagrams show some of the many number patterns within Pascal's triangle, and could be used as a basis for investigation by the children.

Powers of 2							Sum of the numbers in each row	
			1					
		1		1			2	$= 2^1$
		1	2	1			4	$= 2^2$
	1	3	3	1			8	$= 2^3$
	1	4	6	4	1		16	$= 2^4$
1	5	10	10	5	1		32	$= 2^5$
1	6	15	20	15	6	1	64	$= 2^6$

Polygonal numbers

← counting numbers
← triangular numbers
← tetrahedral numbers

```
        1
      1   1
    1   2   1
  1   3   3   1
1   4   6   4   1
1   5  10  10   5   1
1   6  15  20  15   6   1
```

Fibonacci numbers

```
          1
        1      2   (1+1)
      1      3   (1+2)
    1    1    5   (2+3)
  1    2    8   (3+5)
1   3   3   13   (5+8)
1   4   6   4   1
1   5  10  10   5   1
1   6  15  20  15   6   1
```

Essential language
Chance, probability, possible outcomes, distinct outcomes, cases, favourable cases, sample, predict, Quincunx, maze, index rotation, powers, routes.

ATs 1B, 5BC, 9ABC, 14ABC.

Old recipes

Here are a few recipes, taken from a pre-war cookery book, which use Imperial units. They will help the children develop some appreciation of the rough metric equivalents of these measures.

Parkin

What you need
½lb oatmeal
6oz brown sugar
¼lb golden syrup or treacle
½tsp bicarbonate of soda
¼lb flour
¼lb butter
1tsp ground ginger
1tsp mixed spice
Milk for mixing
Pinch of salt
Split almonds for decoration

What to do
● Dissolve the soda in a dessertspoon of milk.
● Mix the oatmeal, flour, salt, ginger, spices and sugar.
● Heat the syrup and fat and stir into the oatmeal mixture.
● Add the soda, and sufficient extra milk to make a stiff mixture.
● Roll into balls.
● Press on to a greased baking sheet and brush with milk.
● Put split almonds on top of each ball.
● Bake for 15 minutes in a hot oven.

Goosenargh cakes

What you need
½lb flour
2oz sugar
Pinch of salt
6oz butter
1 egg yolk
1tsp caraway seeds.

- Cream the butter and sugar, and add the egg yolk gradually.
- Sift the flour and salt, and fold into the mixture. Mix in the caraway seeds.
- Turn out on to a floured board and knead lightly.
- Roll out thinly and cut into rounds.
- Bake in a hot oven for 15 minutes, or until a very pale brown colour.
- Dredge with sugar.

Lemon and ginger biscuits

What you need
½lb flour
1 egg
Rind of 1 lemon
¼lb butter
½lb sugar
½oz ground ginger

What to do
- Sift the flour, sugar and ground ginger.
- Add the grated lemon rind.
- Rub in the butter.
- With the eggs mix to a stiff paste.
- Knead lightly, and roll out thinly.
- Cut into fancy shapes and bake on greased trays for ten minutes in a hot oven, until golden brown.

Knifteh (the Carpet of Allah)
This recipe was invented by Allah Omah 1 in 630 AD.

What you need
4oz butter
4oz blanched sliced almonds
4oz caster sugar
4oz flour
½tsp baking powder
1 tsp rose water
Few drops lemon juice
Pinch of salt

What to do
- Melt the butter.
- Mix all the ingredients together.
- Press smoothly into a greased sandwich tin and bake until a pale golden colour (20 minutes in a moderate oven).

Essential language
Pound (lb), ounce (oz), kilogram (kg), gram (g).

ATs 1AB, 2B, 3B, 8B, 13B.

The power game

This is a game which develops the use and understanding of index notation to express powers of whole numbers. Two to four players can take part.

What you need
Two dice, a calculator.

What to do
The aim is to gain the most points by forming the largest numbers.

Each player in turn rolls both dice. The player selects the score on one of the dice as the whole number and the other score as the index or power of the number. For example, if a player were to roll a five and a six, he or she could choose either 5^6 or 6^5 as a score, aiming to choose the greater number. After choosing their scores, each player calculates his or her score by multiplication, using either a calculator or pencil and paper methods.

A player choosing 5^6 as their score would calculate its value as follows:
$5 \times 5 \times 5 \times 5 \times 5 \times 5 = 15625$

When each player has found the value of their chosen score for that round, these values are compared and the player with the greater number scores one point.

The game ends either after an agreed number of rounds or after an agreed total of points has been won.

Essential language
Index, indices, index notation, power, greater, value, calculate, multiply.

ATs 2A, 3A.

Multiplication snooker

This is a calculator game for two players which involves the multiplication of a three-digit number by a single digit, using the distributive law.

What you need
For each pair of players, one calculator, a six-sided die, a ten-sided die, 15 small counters (the 'reds'), a game board (see page 187) and two score-sheets.

What to do
To start, players roll a die, and the highest throw starts first. The starting player chooses a red, which will have a value of either seven or eight.

For example, Player A might choose a red numbered eight. The next stage is for the player to generate a three-digit number by rolling the ten-sided die three times; for example, Player A might roll seven, two, eight. He or she then has to multiply the number on the ball by the number generated, entering the figures 728×8 into the calculator.

Player A must predict the answer before pressing the equals key, and then calculate the product by using the distributive law, as below:

$$
728 \times 8 \begin{cases} 8 \times 8 - 64 \\ 20 \times 8 - 160 \\ 700 \times 8 - 5600 \end{cases} 5824
$$

This working is checked on the calculator, and if it is correct, Player A then goes on to attempt to pot a 'colour', first rolling the six-sided die to determine the colour to be attempted. If a five is rolled, Player A tries to pot the pink. The ten-sided die is rolled three times as before to generate a three-digit number which must then be multiplied by the ball's number (six in the case of the pink).

After attempting to pot a colour, Player A ends his or her turn and play passes to Player B, who attempts to pot a red and then a colour. If a player misses a red his or her turn ends without attempting to pot a colour.

Points are scored for successful pots as in the game of snooker itself:

red   1 point
yellow   2 points
green   3 points
brown   4 points
blue   5 points
pink   6 points
black   7 points

The player with the greatest number of points either at the end of the game or after an agreed time limit wins the game.

Players keep a record of the game on score-sheets.

Variation

This game may be varied for use at other levels and other stages of ability in multiplication simply by changing the number of throws of the 10-sided die or by changing the numbers on the balls.

Essential language

Multiply, three-digit number, hundreds, tens, units, product, partial product, predict, distributive law.

ATs 3AC.

Division golf

This is a calculator game for two players which provides experience with the identification of factors belonging to equations whose three-digit answers are not exact products; for example, $7 \times ? < 237$. The game gives practice with the 'trial and improve' strategy, and may also be used to illustrate the inverse relationship between multiplication and division.

What you need

For each pair of players, a plan of the golf course, (see page 188) a ten-sided die, a score-sheet each, and a calculator.

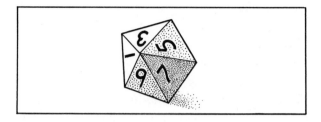

What to do

The aim of the game is to complete a round of the golf course in the least number of strokes. At each hole players throw the ten-sided die to determine their 'club number', which is one of the two factors in the equation.

As marked on the plan of the course, each hole has a given length; a three-digit number which is the equation's answer.

For example, a player who rolled seven at a hole of length 237 would have to solve the equation $7 \times ? < 237$. The aim is to replace ? with the greatest possible number, by means of the 'trial and improve' strategy. Each trial counts as one stroke, and a running total of strokes taken is kept by each player on their score-sheet.

Variation

The game may be varied to suit other levels and teaching stages by changing the lengths of the holes.

Essential language

Equation, factors, product, inverse, trial and improve, greater than, less than.

ATs 3AC, 4AB.

hole	length	club	number sentence	stroke no.	key presses	display	total strokes
1	253	9	$9 \times \square < 253$	1	9 × 30 =	270	
				2	9 × 29 =	261	
			$9 \times 28 < 253$	3	9 × 28 =	252	3
2	412	5	$5 \times \square < 412$	1	5 × 50 =	250	
				2	5 × 90 =	450	
				3	5 × 80 =	400	
			$5 \times 82 < 412$	4	5 × 82 =	410	7

Intercontinental airways

This is a calculator activity in the form of a board game, involving finding differences between positive and negative numbers in the context of temperatures in degrees Celsius. The game may be played by two to four players.

What you need
One set of January temperature/place name cards, counters of different colours, the game board, (see also page 189) a six-sided die and a calculator.

What to do
The players aim to visit each of the six continents; the first to do so is the winner.

To begin the game, players roll the die and the one with the highest score starts.

In this example, Player A begins.

Player A takes the top card from the face-down pack of temperature/place cards, which might be Chicago −2°C.

This determines the player's starting position. The other players then take cards in turn and place their counters in the corresponding positions on the board, returning used cards to the bottom of the pack.

Player A then draws a second card, for example Moscow −11°C. The player then attempts to 'fly' to this city. In order to do so the difference in temperature between Chicago and Moscow must be found. −2°C −? = −11°C

Teachers may wish to provide the children with a temperature scale marked from −45°C to +30°C to help them find the difference between each pair of

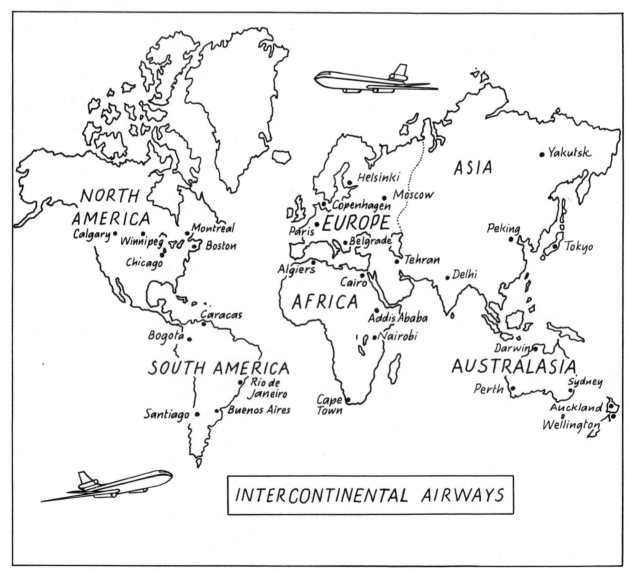

INTERCONTINENTAL AIRWAYS

Helsinki −6°C	Moscow −11°C	Paris +3°C	Belgrade −2°C	Copenhagen 0°C
Peking −4°C	Tehran +1°C	Tokyo +3°C	Yakutsk −43°C	Delhi +14°C
Cairo +13°C	Algiers +11°C	Cape Town +21°C	Nairobi +18°C	Addis Ababa +15°C
Boston −3°C	Chicago −2°C	Calgary −11°C	Montreal −10°C	Winnipeg −20°C
Caracas +12°C	Buenos Aires +23°C	Santiago +19°C	Bogota +14°C	Rio de Janeiro +25°C
Sydney +22°C	Wellington +17°C	Auckland +19°C	Perth +23°C	Darwin +29°C

temperatures.

Player A performs the following operation on the calculator:
$-2 -9 = -11$

A player can only fly to his destination if the answer is correct. If incorrect, he has to try again next time.

Players continue in this way, taking turns, until one of them visits each of the six continents and so wins the game.

Essential language
Temperature, degrees, Celsius, negative, positive, difference, operation, number sentence, equation.

ATs 3D.

Bullseye

This is a division game for two players, which will give children practice with reading a calculator display and approximating to a certain number of decimal places.

What you need
A calculator, about 20 cards with numbers between 100 and 999.

What to do
Place the pack of cards face down. Each player then draws a card from the pack in turn, and enters the number shown into the calculator. They have to try to divide that number by another number to produce an answer as close as possible to a specified number such as 50. Teachers can decide for themselves whether the players should only get one attempt, or whether they can have additional chances to refine their answers. For example:

> PLAYER A
>
> $867 \div 15 = 57 \cdot 8$
>
> $867 \div 16 = 54 \cdot 187$
>
> $867 \div 18 = 48 \cdot 166$
>
> PLAYER B
>
> $431 \div 9 = 47 \cdot 888$
>
> $431 \div 8 = 53 \cdot 875$
>
> $431 \div 8 \cdot 5 = 50 \cdot 705$

Should a player's answer land within a specified zone, such as within 0.25 of the target number, they get five points. Less accurate answers could receive points on a scale like the following:

within 0.25	5 points
within 0.5	points
within 1	3 points
within 2	2 points
within 4	1 point

After ten rounds or so, scores could be totalled to establish the winner. The target number could be altered each time a round is played.

Essential language
Tenth, hundredth, thousandth.

ATs 1ABC, 4AB.

Level 5 glossary of terms

The following glossary explains some of the mathematical terms which are contained within the statements of attainment for mathematics at Level 5.

Analyse
To examine the gathered data in order to draw conclusions.

Collate
To bring together and place in order so that comparisons may be made.

Congruence
The property of shapes which are identical in shape and size, irrespective of position.

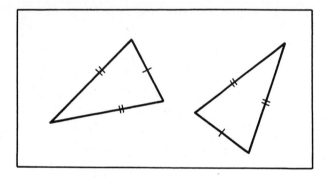

Continuous data
Information concerning continuous variables, ie those that are not separate, such as length, time, weight, etc., where the 'in-between' values have real meaning.

Conversion graph
A straight line graph which compares two related units, usually from two different systems of measurement; eg kilograms and pounds, litres and gallons, kilometres and miles.

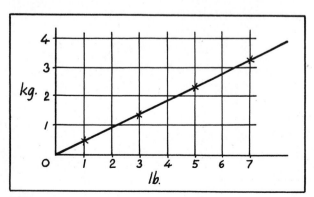

Coordinates in all four quadrants
Coordinates in which the numbers in each ordered pair may be either positive or negative, their positions being either above or below the x-axis and to the left or right of the y-axis.

Cube
To raise a number to the third power; for example, 4 cubed (4^3) is produced by $4\times4\times4=64$.

Cube root
The inverse process to raising a number to a cube; for example, if 4 cubed (4^3) is 64, then the cube root of 64 is 4.

Factors
Whole numbers which will divide exactly into another whole number; for example, 1, 12, 2, 6, 3 and 4 are the factors of 12.

Index notation
The method of indicating the power of a number; eg $2\times2\times2$, or 2 to the third power, is written as 2^3 in index notation, where the ^{3} is the index indicating the power.

Multiples
Numbers having a stated whole number as a factor; eg 40, 32, 28 and 18 all have 2 as a factor, therefore they are all multiples of 2.

Networks
A diagram consisting of junctions called nodes joined by lines referred to as arcs. Such diagrams are often used to solve problems concerned with routes.

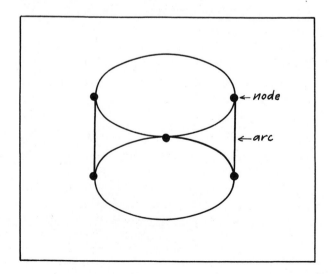

Observation sheet

A table or chart constructed for the collection of certain observed data.

Powers of ten

A power (see index notation) indicates how many times a number is to be multiplied by itself. So the powers of ten are $10^1 = 10$, $10^2 = 100$ (10×10), $10^3 = 1000$ ($10 \times 10 \times 10$), and so on.

Prime numbers

Any whole number that has only two factors, itself and 1, is said to be a prime number. The number 1 is not regarded as a prime number as it only has one factor.

Ratio

A comparison of two quantities by expressing one as a fraction of the other; for example, the ratio of 1cm to 5cm can be expressed as 1:5, where the sign : represents 'to' or 'is to'. A unitary ratio is one where the first term of the ratio is 1, as in the above example and in scales quoted on Ordnance Survey maps; eg 1:25 000 and 1:50 000.

Significant figures

The digits in a number that are acceptable as an approximation. The following digits are accepted as being significant:
• Each digit which is not zero, eg 3.
• Each zero digit between other digits, eg 304.
• Each zero digit which is not used solely to indicate the position of the decimal point, eg 304.3061.

For example, 487.5 to three significant figures is 487 and 0.2041 to 3 significant figures is 0.204 (the zero in the units place is not a significant figure, but the zero in the second place of decimals is).

Spatial arrangements

Arranging counters, for example, in the form of a polygon, in order to develop polygonal numbers. Arranging counters in the form of a triangle will produce triangular numbers.

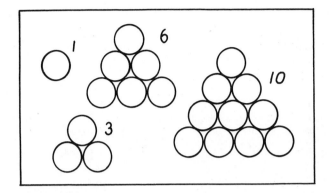

Squared

A number raised to the second power by being multiplied by itself, eg 6 squared (6^2) is $6 \times 6 = 36$.

Square root

A number which when raised to the second power will produce another given number. A square root of 16 is 4, because $4^2 = 16$. Another square root of 16 is -4. Thus, each number has two square roots.

Trial and improve methods

A problem-solving strategy which involves the following stages:
• Make a realistic trial.
• Check the result of the trial against the conditions of the problem.
• Use the information gained from the result of the first trial to make an improved trial.
• Continue this procedure until the solution is found.

This procedure may be summarised in the form of a flow chart.

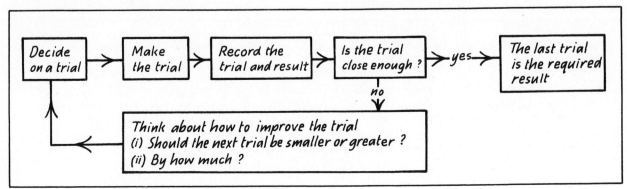

Level 5: Programme of Study

This diagram shows how the programme of study can be expanded, suggesting teaching stages where applicable.

- Investigate square and cubic numbers.
- Relate index notation to place value in base ten.
- Investigate the powers of numbers other than ten.

- Compare two lengths using ratios.
- Draw diagrams to scale using unitary ratios.
- Represent ratios by drawing line graphs.
- Calculate unitary ratios.

Using and applying mathematics
- Select the materials and the mathematics to use for a task; check there is sufficient information; work methodically and review progress.
- Interpret mathematical information presented in oral, written or visual form.
- Make and test simple statements.

- Convert fractions to percentages and vice versa.
- Calculate a fraction of a set of objects.
- Calculate a percentage of a set of objects.

Number
- Use index notation to express powers of whole numbers.
- Use unitary ratios.
- Understand and use non-calculator methods by which a three-digit number is multiplied by a two-digit number and a three-digit number is divided by a two-digit number.
- Calculate fractions and percentages of quantities.
- Multiply and divide mentally single-digit multiples of powers of ten.
- Use negative numbers in context.
- Use 'trial and improvement' methods.
- Approximate, using significant figures or decimal places.

- Multiply and divide multiples of 100 by single-digit numbers.
- Multiply and divide two-digit numbers by two-digit numbers, using extended notation and cubes to count with in the early stages.
- Investigate and try out tests of divisibility.

- In your head, multiply multiples of ten by 100.
- Mentally divide multiples of 100 by ten.
- In your head, multiply multiples of ten by multiples of 100.
- Mentally divide multiples of 100 by multiples of ten.

- Relate negative numbers to a temperature scale, the goal difference on a football league table, etc.
- Relate negative numbers to a number line, and use the line to add and subtract with them.
- Practise adding and subtracting negative numbers in everyday situations.

Algebra
- Understand and use terms such as 'prime', 'square', 'cube', 'square root', 'cube root', 'multiple' and 'factor'.
- Generate sequences.
- Recognise patterns in numbers through spatial arrangements.
- Understand and use simple formulae or equations expressed in symbolic form.
- Express simple functions symbolically.
- Understand and use coordinates in all four quadrants.

- Revise the position value of digits in numbers with up to two decimal places.
- Practise rounding up and rounding down to the nearest ten, 100 etc.
- Write numbers to one or two decimal places.
- Introduce the concepts of significant figures and 'place holders' in relation to accuracy.
- Write numbers to a given number of significant figures.

- Develop skills of estimation and approximation.
- Make a sensible first trial.
- Use information from the previous trial to decide upon the next trial.

Level 5: Programme of Study (continued)

● Understand and use simple scales such as 1cm to 1m, 10cm to 1km.
● Understand and use simple ratio scales such as 1:2, 1:10 etc.
● Understand and use more complex ratio scales such as those used by the Ordnance Survey.

● Know the relationships between metric measures.
● Convert one metric unit into two metric units, eg 324cm = 3m 24cm.
● Convert one metric unit into a decimal fraction of another metric unit, eg 324cm = 3.24m.

● Understand the terms 'congruent' and 'similar'.
● Understand the differences between congruent and similar shapes.
● Sort subsets of congruent shapes from a set of shapes.
● List the corresponding parts of congruent shapes.

● Investigate the axes of symmetry of various polygons.
● Investigate the orders of rotational symmetry of various polygons.
● Look at translations, reflections and rotations within tessellations of polygons.

● Practise using coordinates in the first quadrant.
● Plot points in all four quadrants from given coordinates.
● Give coordinates of points appearing in all four quadrants.

Measures
● Understand the notion of scale in maps and drawings.
● Use Imperial units still in daily use and know their rough metric equivalents.
● Convert one metric unit to another.
● Measure and draw angles to the nearest degree.

Shape and space
● Understand congruence of simple shapes.
● Use properties associated with intersecting and parallel lines and triangles and know associated language.
● Identify the symmetries of various shapes.
● Use networks to solve problems.
● Specify location by means of coordinates in four quadrants.

Handling data
● Design and use an observation sheet to collect data; collate and analyse results.
● Collect and group continuous data and create frequency tables.
● Insert and interrogate data in a computer database and draw conclusions.
● Construct and interpret pie charts from a collection of data with a few variables.
● Construct and interpret conversion graphs.
● Construct and interpret frequency diagrams and choose class intervals for a continuous variable.
● Distinguish between estimates of probabilities based on statistical evidence and those based on assumptions of symmetry.
● Know that if each of n events is assumed to be equally likely, the probability of one occurring is $1/n$.
● Know that different outcomes may result from repeating an experiment.

● Examine packaging that uses both metric and Imperial measures.
● Compare metric and Imperial measures to develop the idea of equivalence.
● Recognise the units which are in everyday use – pints of milk, pounds of potatoes, litres and gallons of petrol, metres of cloth, kilograms of sugar.

● Put angles in order by estimation.
● Know how to use a protractor properly.
● Estimate and measure angles to the nearest ten degrees.
● Estimate and measure angles to the nearest degree.
● Draw given angles using ruler and protractor, estimating first by sketching.
● Construct shapes from given angles.

● Know the properties of opposite and adjacent angles of intersecting lines.
● Understand the properties of triangles.

● Understand the terms 'network', 'arc' and 'node'.
● Investigate the traversability of networks and relate this to Euler's theorem.
● Find out the shortest routes using networks.
● Investigate the relationship between arcs, nodes and regions in a network.

Level 5 : attainment targets 1–8

Use this chart to check which attainment targets are covered by each activity.

ACTIVITY	1 A	1 B	1 C	2 A	2 B	3 A	3 B	3 C	3 D	4 A	4 B	5 A	5 B	5 C	6 A	6 B	7	8 A	8 B	8 C	8 D
Planning a visit	●	●					●												●	●	
Create a game	●	●								●								●		●	
Fitness	●																			●	
In the news		●					●														
Family budgets	●	●				●	●		●		●										
Off the shelf	●	●					▲				●										
Miles per gallon	●	●			●						●							●	▲		
Old money and measures	●	●					●				●								▲	●	
Digit shift		●							▲					●							
LOGO activities								●	●						●	▲					
Tessellation																					
Mystic roses	●	●	●									●	●		●	●					
The sieve of Eratosthenes	●	●	●									▲	●	●							
Polygonal numbers	●	●	●									●	▲	●							
Regular polygons															●	●					▲
Transformations																	●				
Channel crossing	●	●	●							▲				●	▲	●		●			
Networks									●						●	●					
Pascal's triangle		●											●	●							
Old recipes	●	●			●	●													▲		
The power game				▲		●															
Multiplication snooker						▲		●													
Division golf						●		●		▲	●										
Intercontinental airways									▲												
Bullseye	●	●	●							▲	▲										

Key: ● = touches on
▲ = especially
relevant

Level 5 : attainment targets 9–14

Use this chart to check which attainment targets are covered by each activity.

ACTIVITY	9 A	9 B	9 C	10 A	10 B	11 A	11 B	11 C	12 A	12 B	12 C	13 A	13 B	13 C	14 A	14 B	14 C
Planning a visit									•								
Create a game																	
Fitness	•	•							•	•	•		•	•			
In the news	•	•							▲	•		•		•			
Family budgets	•	•										▲					
Off the shelf										•							
Miles per gallon									•				▲				
Old money and measures	•	•										•	•				
Digit shift																	
LOGO activities				•	•	•		▲									
Tessellation				•	▲	•											
Mystic roses						•											
The sieve of Eratosthenes																	
Polygonal numbers																	
Regular polygons					•	•											
Transformations				•		•		▲									
Channel crossing																	
Networks	•	•	•				▲										
Pascal's triangle	•	•	•												•	▲	▲
Old recipes												•					
The power game																	
Multiplication snooker																	
Division golf																	
International airways																	
Bullseye																	

Key: • = touches on
▲ = especially
relevant

Level 5 : Contexts

This chart shows the wider contexts of each activity.

ACTIVITY	Everyday situations	Everyday problems	Games and fun	Maths problems	Maths investigations	Calculator activities	Computer activities	English	Science	Art	PE	History	Geography	Music	Technology	Local Curriculum	RE	Possible topic link	School-wide themes
Planning a visit		•				•							•			•		•	•
Create a game			•								•								
Fitness			•				•		•		•							•	
In the news	•							•								•		•	
Family budgets	•					•										•		•	•
Off the shelf						•							•			•		•	•
Miles per gallon				•		•							•			•		•	•
Old money and measures												•						•	
Digit shift					•	•													
LOGO activities							•			•									
Tessellation					•					•									
Mystic roses					•		•			•									
The sieve of Eratosthenes					•														
Polygonal numbers					•		•												
Regular polygons					•					•									
Transformations					•														
Channel crossing			•										•						•
Networks			•				•					•	•						
Pascal's triangle					•									•					
Old recipes	•								•			•						•	•
The power game			•	•															
Multiplication snooker			•			•													
Division golf			•			•													
Intercontinental airways			•		•								•					•	•
Bullseye			•			•													

Squirrel run, see page 58

J
I
H
G
F
E
D
C
B
A
Start

Hop it, see page 59

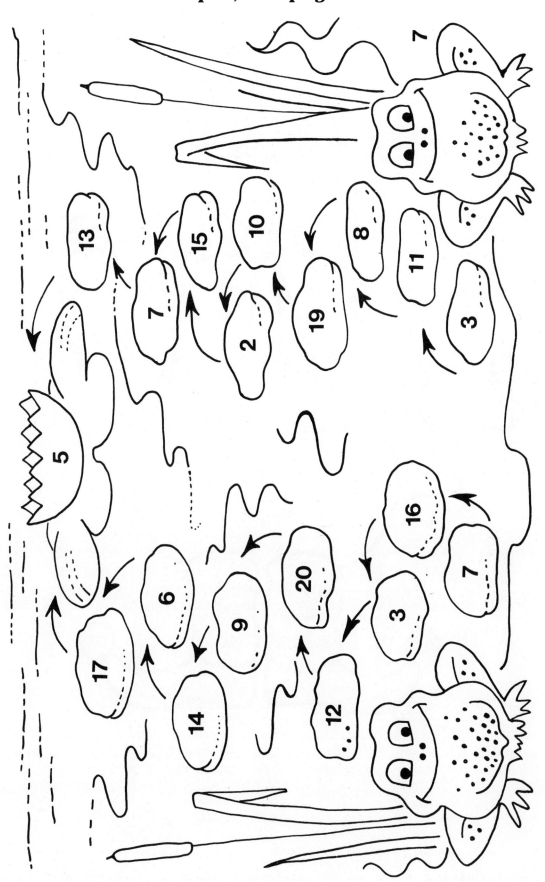

Buy a juggler, see page 61

Buy a juggler, see page 61

Escape from Planet X, see page 92

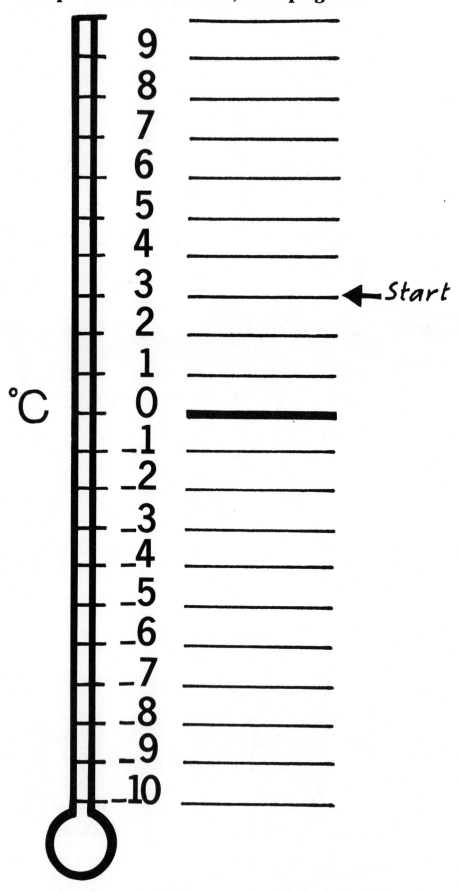

←Start

Downhill run, see page 94

Fill in the flags with different numbers to vary the game.

Hexangle, see page 95

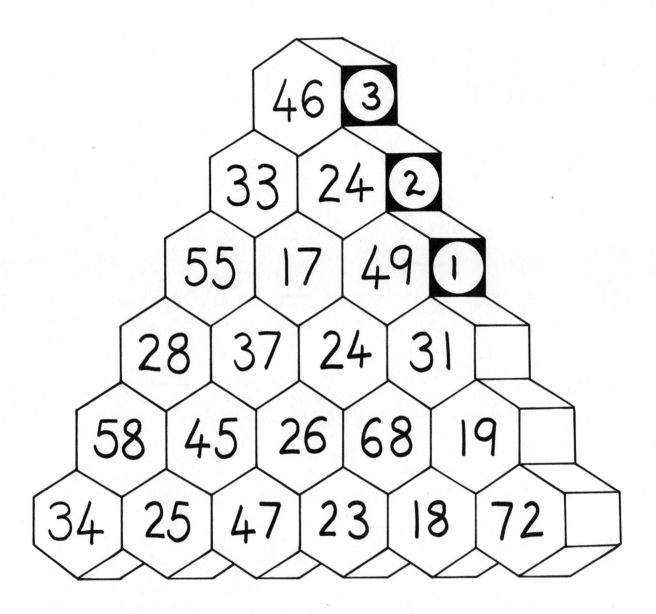

Along the dragon's back, see page 130

Fill in the spaces with different numbers to vary the game.

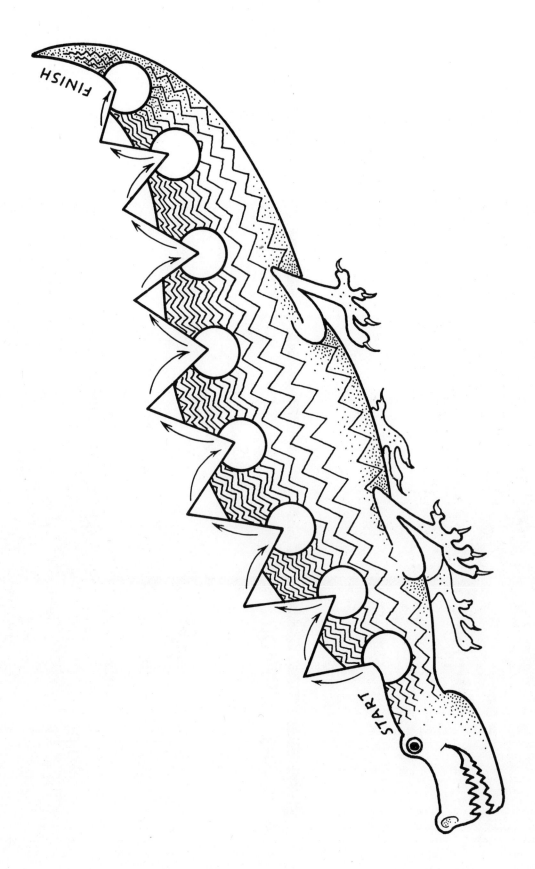

FINISH

START

Channel crossing, see page 156

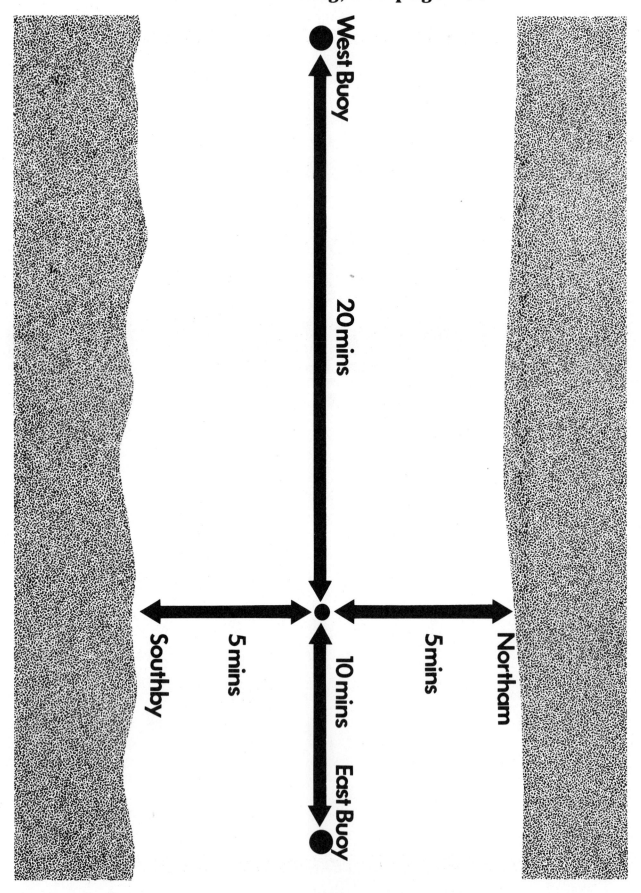

Multiplication snooker, see page 166

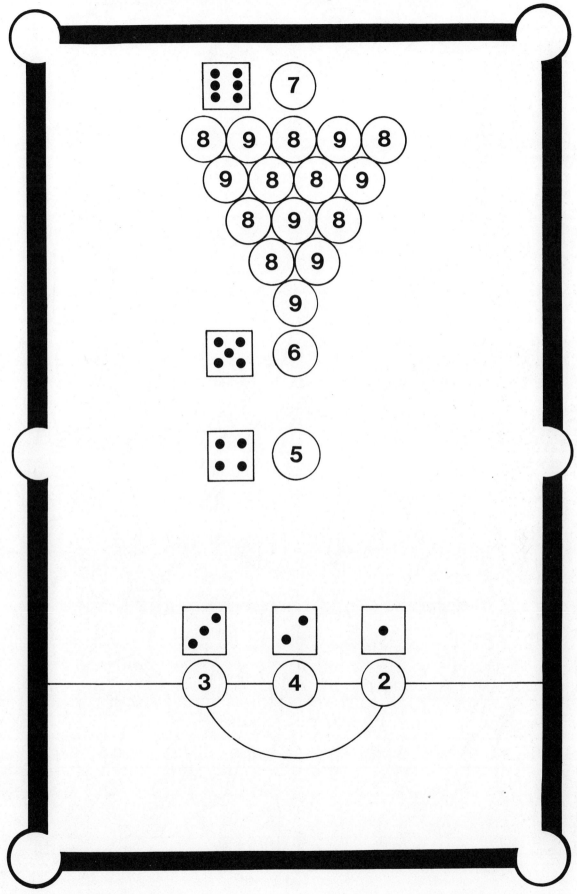

Division golf, see page 167

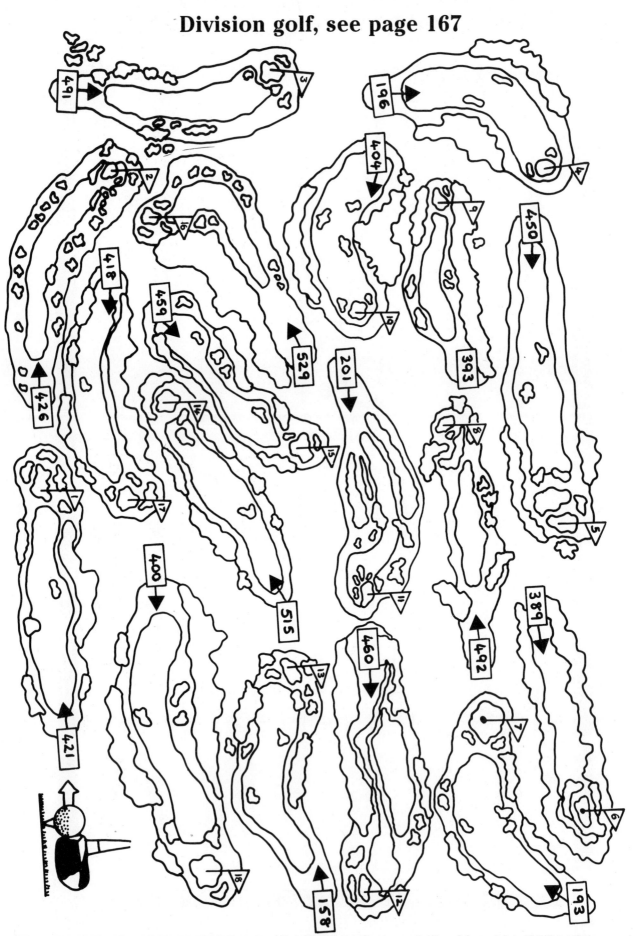

Intercontinental airways, see page 168

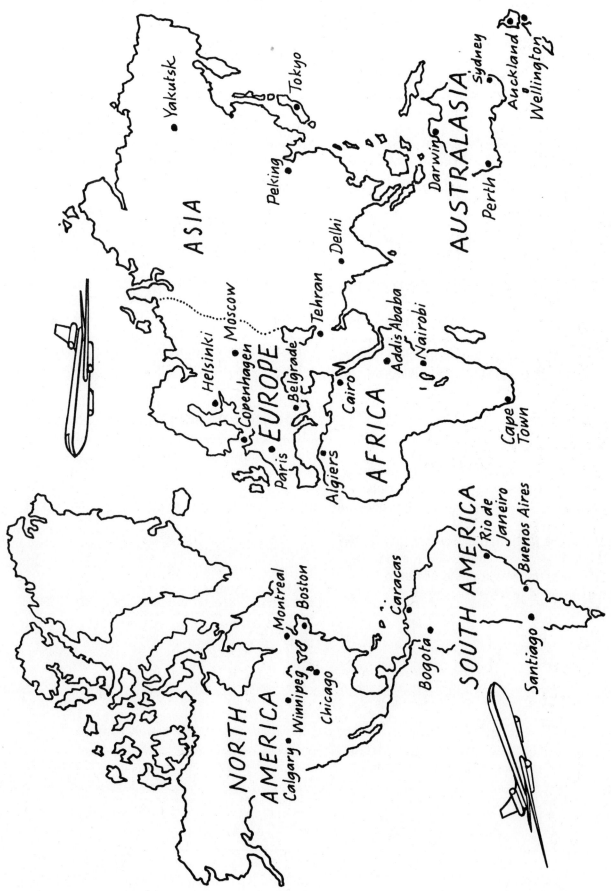

Other Scholastic books

Bright Ideas

The Bright Ideas books provide a wealth of resources for busy primary school teachers. There are now more than 20 titles published, providing clearly explained and illustrated ideas on topics ranging from *Word Games* and *Science* to *Display* and *Classroom Management*. Each book contains material which can be photocopied for use in the classroom.

Bright Ideas for Early Years

The *Bright Ideas for Early Years* series has been written specially for nursery and reception teachers, playgroup leaders and all those who work with 3 to 6-year-olds. The books provide sound practical advice on all areas of learning. The ideas and activities are easy to follow and clearly illustrated.

Teacher Handbooks

The Teacher Handbooks give an overview of the latest research in primary education, and show how it can be put into practice in the classroom. Covering all the core areas of the curriculum, the *Teacher Handbooks* are indispensable to the new teacher as a source of information and useful to the experienced teacher as a quick reference guide.

Management Books

The Management Books are designed to help teachers to organise their time, classroom and teaching more efficiently. The books deal with topical issues, such as *Parents and Schools* and organising and planning *Project Teaching*, and are written by authors with lots of practical advice and experiences to share.

Let's Investigate

Let's Investigate is an exciting range of photocopiable maths activity books giving open-ended investigative tasks. The series will complement and extend any existing maths programme. Designed to cover the 6 to 12-year-old age range these books are ideal for small group or individual work. Each book presents progressively more difficult concepts and many of the activities can be adapted for use throughout the primary school. Detailed teacher's notes outlining the objectives of each photocopiable sheet and suggesting follow-up activities have been included.